Year-Round

W·R·E·A·T·H·S

Year-Round
W·R·E·A·T·H·S

Creative Ideas for Every Season

RICHARD KOLLATH
Photographs by BRUCE McCANDLESS

Facts On File
New York • Oxford

A FRIEDMAN GROUP BOOK

First published in 1992 by
Facts On File, Inc.
460 Park Avenue South
New York, New York 10016

Library of Congress Cataloging-in-Publication Data
Kollath, Richard.
      Year-round wreaths: creative ideas for every
season / Richard Kollath : edited by Carol Spier ;
photographs by Bruce McCandless.
            p.   cm.
      Includes index.
      ISBN 0-8160-2601-7
      1. Wreaths.   I. Title.
SB449.5.W74K63   1992
745.92—dc20   91-32957
                                                              CIP

Facts On File books are available at special
discounts when purchased in
bulk quantities for businesses, associations,
institutions or sales promotions.
Please call our Special Sales Department in New
York at 212/683-2244
(dial 800/322-8755 except in NY, AK or HI).

YEAR-ROUND WREATHS
was prepared and produced by
Michael Friedman Publishing Group, Inc.
15 West 26th Street
New York, New York 10010

Editor: Carol Spier
Art Director: Jeff Batzli
Designer: Charles Donahue
Typeset by Bookworks Plus
Color separation by Excel Graphic Arts Ltd.
Printed and bound in Hong Kong by Leefung-
Asco Printers Ltd.

1   3   5   7   9   10   8   6   4   2

Dedication

I dedicate this book to Bert and Di Di Carpenter, with love and gratitude for the richness and depth
they have brought to my life.

Acknowledgments

*This book of wreaths has come into being through the good will and talents of many friends and associates. It is with my deepest
appreciation that I acknowledge their invaluable contributions.*

To Michael Friedman and Karla Olson of the Friedman Publishing Group for giving me the opportunity to do this
second book of wreaths and for providing me with their absolute trust and support, many thanks.

To Carol Spier, who worked with great care and patient understanding in editing the text.
For all her contributions, my warmest thanks.

To Jeff Batzli, Charles Donahue, and the design and production departments at the Friedman Group for allowing me
the freedom to develop the images within the book. I appreciate their support.

To Bruce McCandless, a very talented photographer and good friend, whose sensitive control with his camera
provided all the images for this book. Working with you is such a pleasure.

To my father and mother who were so helpful in providing encouragement and who sent box after box of dried
materials from their Florida landscape. For all of their much appreciated efforts, my thanks.

*I wish to thank the friends and neighbors who allowed their homes and gardens to be photographed, who were generous with the loan of
accessories and contribution of time.*

To Robert Palmatier and Fredric Misner of Thumbprint Antiques, thanks for all the charm and treasures
of your wonderful shop.

To Daniel Ross of R. Ross & Sons Nursery, for always stocking the best of the season.

To Arthur and Elizabeth Weyhe for sharing the glories of their country house and landscape.

To Richard and Nadia Kirgan, friends and neighbors who have a good way with wood.
For your time and efforts, many thanks.

To Jane Schneider, for her generous contribution.

*And my thanks to the many people in the floral, crafts and decorating trades, without whose prompt and patient assistance this book
would have been so difficult:* Barbara Register of Knud Nielsen; Nancy Presley of Bob's Candy Company; Aleene Eckstein
of Artis, Inc; Robert Hand of Arrow Fastener Co., Inc; Erica Gjersvik of Pangaea; Ursel Thiergart of Brimar, Inc; Sherry
Timbrook of Hallmark Cards, Inc; John Riccardi and Rudy Grant of Seagroatt Floral Co; Sondra Bogunia of Stone
Fleck; Bob MacLeod and Steve Byckeiwicz of Kiss My Face; Phil Burruss of Vaban Ribbons International;
Lana Wechsler and Jean Bates of Just Accents; Elli Schneider of the Offray Ribbon Co; John Melton of
MPR Associates; and Fred Sutton, who makes such beautiful silk flowers.

CONTENTS

PREFACE

When I was a child, my father and grandfather planted the most inspired gardens. Linear in design, they bordered terraces and marked our pathways with color. Some areas of these plantings, where hybrid dahlias rose as tall as my grandfather and towering delphiniums swept the sky with graceful rhythms, dwarfed my perspective of the landscape. Others, where marigolds and geraniums, zinnias and coxcomb pulsed vibrantly in the summer heat, made me gasp with the wonder of pure color. Within each planting there was a predominant theme, one that clearly established the scale of the plants and the palette. What I remember now about those lush arrangements was that there were unexpected juxtapositions, genuine surprises—an unusual accent of color or a discreet blend of textures that commanded attention within the thematic order. Other elements from nature would appear among the flowers—a log bench tucked in beneath shrubs and vines, various mosses covering slate walks or shaded patios. Boulders, silent along the side of the fish pond, were surrounded by lily-of-the-valley that spread from the edge of the water to the deep shade of thickening trees. I liked seeing those surprises and in time I grew to understand them—to comprehend the poetry, romance, and wonder brought forth by the skillful and visionary guidance of my family.

Early on in life I had the opportunity to live in a horticultural environment where flowers graced and ruled my every day. There were greenhouses devoted to orchids, others filled seasonally with the autumnal shades of chrysanthemums, or the vivid red of poinsettias. Deep underground my father had a room for keeping spring bulbs. There, on shelves, wooden flats and clay pots were filled with tulips and daffodils and sweet fragrant hyacinths. As seasons came and passed so did colors. Each cycle brought new life to our landscape. I remember those singular changes with vividness. The triumph of all this was the way fresh flowers were brought into our home, the manner in which my mother took many unexpected assortments of garden blooms, and whether by whim or design, brought them magically together. There was a sense of grace and spontaneity about her arrangements, and it was wonderful how each flower held its character in the midst of the rest.

As this was part of my life then, it is a part of my life today. Now my summer garden ripples with color and fragrance, the woods abound with grape and bittersweet vines. The attic in my home holds screen trays for drying flowers, and from the rafters above these I hang inverted bunches of freshly picked blooms. Plastic sweater boxes hold desiccating silica gel, which gently dries the heads of flowers. Each drying session evokes a harvest, each harvest a slice in the cycle of my life. Thus focused, I have led an incredibly rich and productive life.

What I have realized is that from those early flower-filled experiences I learned a great deal about design; about space, color, and proportion. How in fact to assemble an assortment of elements, how to explore and become comfortable with the tensions between the forms. How to impose order on my materials, and when to be ordered about by them. To find excitement in this work, and to develop a personal design vocabulary. Most valuable of all, to take chances and break the rules.

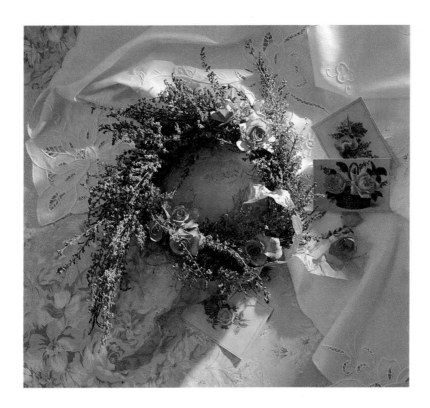

INTRODUCTION

YEAR-ROUND WREATHS is a book of ideas, a creative source from which to learn and whence to advance. I hope you will find it a stepping-stone on your path of creativity and self-expression, and that by looking at it and reading it you will find your own design vocabulary. I have worked with many materials to create over seventy wreaths; they are seasonal, festive, functional, whimsical, and even silly. I have tried to infuse each one with a unique beauty that I discovered through the process of handling and composing the elements that adorn it.

This is a book filled with ideas that are meant to be adapted and interpreted personally rather than literally. There is plenty of practical, technical information in the last chapter that will answer any questions you may have as to how best to construct a particular sort of wreath or use some less familiar materials; and while I want very much for you to feel confident about the precise work involved, I am much more excited to think that you may be inspired by the first three chapters to work in new creative directions, to think about design, nature, materials, color, texture, composition, and also sen-

timent. It is my hope that your wreath making will be enriched by this book and that you will adapt some of the suggestions, allowing them to become a part of your personal style and creative rhythm.

With this in mind I have written not only about how I made the wreaths but how I designed them, where I found my inspiration, why I arranged the components as I did, which aesthetic principles influenced my creative processes. I have written that I did this or that, found such and such to be true, or experienced a particular reaction, and I encourage you to recognize similar feelings in yourself when you turn your hands to wreath making or any other creative pursuit. There is no one right way to design, but there are certain factors and concepts that affect the successful execution of each idea; they are abstract but important and if kept in mind as you work, will provide a frame of reference in which you can examine questions.

As in painting or drawing, the art of wreath design involves principles of space, form, color, texture, movement, and scale; in bringing balance to these you create a design that is pleasing. As you work, you will find that each composition on a

wreath base has a line to it, and within the linear arrangement of objects there is movement. You can enhance this quality by changing the relative scale of the decorative elements, or by altering the arrangement of the colors, or by juxtaposing disparate textures; usually you will be concerned with all of these. The way you work with these concepts lets you control the movement and depth in your design; lets you decide whether you want to create something energetic or sedate, formal, fey, lighthearted, or sentimental. As you come to understand these influences you begin to see the things that make one design special while another is prosaic, and this is the great challenge and wonderful mystery of creativity. For there are no strict or definable rules, and in the end, the judgment is purely subjective.

When I begin to design a wreath, I ask myself a series of questions. Such questions determine much about the development of the piece in hand. What size; how I will treat the surface; questions about color, use of materials; and detailed thoughts about the manipulation of specific elements pass through my mind: Does the wreath have an intended use or is it simply a celebration of flowers or pinecones? Do I wish to impose order on my materials or let them guide my hands?

If you analyze the creative premises of wreath making you will see that the designer accepts a conventional form—most often the circle—as a given that he will use to make an aesthetic statement, a visual poem or song. In contrast to the limited shape with which he begins he may choose among virtually limitless materials to effect the transformation he has in mind. When you accept

this dichotomy and examine the possibilities you inevitably make decisions; choices that in effect become the vocabulary with which you work. As your vocabulary grows and you become comfortable using it, you feel yourself in control of the creative process and are able to work beyond the obvious and explore the abstract.

There may or may not be a pattern to the way you begin, but through the process many paths are explored. When you are developing designs your imagination will suggest concepts and solve problems, and it is very important to become comfortable trusting it. On the other hand, even the most fertile imagination needs some nourishment, and it is a fine idea to keep an inspirational file of clippings, photos, materials, samples, and colors. When you make this file, don't cheat yourself by including only things that are obviously wreath-related, but put in anything that ignites your imagination. Anything that intrigues you is worth filing; someday it may give you just the nudge you need to try something different or solve a particular problem.

Some thoughts in brief:

• Your first concern may be location or function. Do you want to make a wreath to adorn a specific place or to suit a special occasion? If the first is true (and all designs ultimately benefit from your knowledge of where they will hang), then take a moment to understand the location—the other things in it, the colors that are there, and the space to be filled. It would be a disappointment to squeeze a generous wreath into a small space or find that in a large expanse you were losing a miniature one. If you are making a wreath for an occasion, decide if there is a theme or convention that you wish to observe. This may indicate the use of certain materials or send you to your clipping file for some stylistic inspiration.

• The materials with which you wish to work will have a great deal to say about how you proceed. What kind of base will you begin with? How will you hold the elements together? Gather all of your materials before you begin and think about the ways they relate to one another, make experimental placements, look at the negative space as well as that which is filled with various flowers, pods, cones, and greens. Is the effect interesting, is it boring, can you balance it, is something missing, what makes it unusual?

• Examine the relative proportions of the elements that you plan to use. If some of the materials you choose are way out of scale with the others, they may destroy your final composition. Not all elements should be of the same size, but their relationship should be pleasing, and any dramatic shifts in scale should be meaningful.

• Color is always important to think about and understand; it is very often the first thing the viewer will perceive and sets the mood as nothing else does. Study the mixing of colors, check the blending of the tones of a particular palette. Experimentation is wonderful and I strongly suggest that it be done, but I encourage you to work out your color scheme before you start to assemble a piece, to be sure that it works and that you have the necessary elements. As you look at color, think about the texture of your materials as well, for texture affects the reflection of light—which is what color is—and various tactile surfaces can alter the mood of a composition.

This advice is not meant to sound forbidding. I simply feel that it is so important to be aware of what is happening when you work. Even simple changes can completely transform mood—observe this as you work. When you place one flower against another, you are linking the principles of proportion, color, texture, and form; when you do this with care, with intention, poetry, energy, and wit, you are realizing your creative potential. But most importantly, you should enjoy the process, have a good time, be open to new ideas, and recognize your own powers—confidence follows practice.

Wreath making is one of the kindest creative endeavors you can undertake, as it involves so many wonderful connections with nature and allows so much freedom of expression. It is not a difficult craft, so you should experience not frustration but many hours of rewarding pleasure. Create for yourself, allow your imagination to be free, and with that freedom bring forth creations that reflect your sensibilities and challenge your abilities. The road is open to all, and the essential guideposts are within these pages. Travel well and with good luck.

CHAPTER

1

WREATHS THROUGHOUT
THE HOME

There is such an energy in the early stages of autumn, when the sky is clear, the air is sharp, and the countryside is full of activity. The garden gets harvested, the leaves turn and then fall, and the vines that fill the stone walls begin to show their berries. I always plan an autumn hike or two in order to gather a supply of bittersweet and rose hips for the wreaths I make.

Bittersweet, with its brilliant berries and great, gesturing vines, is a singular plant. Every autumn I make from it a simple wreath and a naturally falling swag for my front door. I take the longest runners, weave some of them into a loose circle to make the wreath base, then add shorter vines to the growing ring until it takes on a rich fullness. Because bittersweet grows in a particularly wild, cascading manner, it seems right to allow the ends of each length to remain free. I like to carry this spirit to the swag, draping the vines much as I found them in the woods. I place some nails around the doorframe and then simply wire the vines to them. I might include additional elements gleaned on woodland walks: a bird's nest, pinecones, or lichen-covered twigs.

Hanging to one side of the door, the wreath is protected from the bumps of comings and goings so the berries will stay on the vines as they dry. However, the birds love to eat them, and if I leave it too long it will be barren. Before that happens, I often move the wreath indoors, where its vivid color will last well into the winter as a gentle reminder of seasons passing.

Moving a wreath from one location to another, whether to protect it or just to effect a change, can put a new perspective on its design. Although ideally a wreath is designed to complement its hanging place you can sometimes discover new spaces that show it to advantage. I often move my designs around—from outdoors to inside, from a bright room to a quiet one—to see whether and how effectively they hold up in different environments.

Last year, when I removed the bittersweet wreath from my front entry to save it from the birds, I hung it on a cupboard in my kitchen, where it brought a warmth to the pale neutral colors in the room.

This repositioning of the wreath was a simple way to extend its use; a recycling, if you will, but more than a repetition. Seen against a new surrounding, it commanded fresh responses and a new appreciation.

utumn is one of the most fruitful times of the year for me. The abundant harvest has such a rich array of potential design materials; I can explore and experiment at will. Not only are the seasonal colors naturally harmonious, there are wonderful textures to be found in drying leaves and maturing produce.

This large seasonal wreath is alive with movement; the light colors bounce against the deep tones, and the spiked shape of the leaves and corn husks spring away from the surface. For its base I used a loose coil of grapevine. I dotted small ears of Indian corn around it in a random pattern, tying them on with strands of raffia, double-knotted and left long to trail over the surface. I inserted clusters of gold, deep rust, and bronze oak leaves between the corn ears, repeating the rhythmic play of their dark and light colors and setting off the pale husks. This contrast was further emphasized with the addition of light-colored gourds and dark pinecones, which pull the eye in and out of the surface.

When you select gourds, which are plentiful at this time of year, choose them for their appealing colors and shapes, keeping an eye out for those with good, strong stems that will be easy to wire onto florists' picks. Should the stems break, you can hot-glue the gourds onto the picks, using a little moss to reinforce the bond. When your composition is arranged to your satisfaction, use hot glue to secure the picks to the grapevine.

o matter where I am, I find my creative sensibilities challenged by the sight of materials that could possibly be used in wreath making. This constant questioning—what would this do, how could that become part of a new wreath?—makes my shopping excursions and rambles through the countryside as pleasurable as the time spent putting the designs together. I never stop thinking of the aesthetic qualities of the materials that catch my eye or—since the unexpected will ultimately make all the difference between an obvious and/or inventive design—of unusual or surprising ways to work with or enhance them.

In the autumn, farm stands abound with Indian corn, gourds, dried pods, and flowers. It seems that every time you go there is something new to consider. One day I saw an enticingly generous bunch of yellow corn hanging at a local farm stand and liked its elegant simplicity. I felt the corn would complement a wreath I was making of gold, yellow, and orange flowers, so I bought it.

I had already covered a straw base with straw flowers, yarrow, orange thistles, and lanterns, organizing them in separate bands so their colors and textures were distinct. My intention was to hang the bunch of corn on the wreath; as I explored this idea I felt that a long vertical garland would give the so-far compact design that sought-after element of surprise. I separated the corn into small clusters and hung them from the base with some wire. The naturally pale corn husks stand out against the saturated harvest colors, and the bright yellow tumbles rhythmically out of the wreath and down the cascade of the garland.

s I work I am continually aware of the relationship of the color and texture of my materials to the composition as a whole. This sensitivity guides me as I shape a sometimes complex mix of materials into a design that flows rhythmically and yet invites the eye to rest here and there to acknowledge the parts that comprise the whole. I generally try not to make my wreath symmetrical, as I feel that symmetry, especially in a circular format, is less interesting to the observer—predictable and therefore less enjoyable. This is not to say that there is no pattern or scheme—certainly a pleasing design has balance and order—but that my tendency is to enjoy the creative process and keep the rules loose, to be receptive to anything the materials may have to show me. I am always experimenting, trying variations, examining possibilities.

I am sometimes nearly beset with the need to take advantage of the fabulous array of raw materials in the autumn, to express my great sense of appreciation. In making this lush harvest wreath I wanted to capture the warmth and fullness of what is to me the richest time of year. Dark pinecones, textured sunflowers, velvety coxcombs, and small, bright tansy flowers nestled in a dense bed of leaves seem to express perfectly the range and beauty of the season.

Though this wreath appears abundant and complex, it was really very simply constructed. I began by gluing or wiring all of the decorative elements to florists' picks so that they would be easy to position on the straw base. I established the bed of leaves, simply scattering them in an irregular arrangement around the ring, choosing each for the variations in its color, and adding a few dark green galax leaves to contrast the livelier oak. Once the background was roughed in I added the larger elements: first the sunflowers and then the coxcomb and pinecones. (Sunflowers become a little delicate when dry so you need to take some care when handling them.) With the bigger pieces placed among the leaves, I began to fill in some of the negative space in the design with other dried materials—always standing back as I worked to judge the overall effect—and adding German statice, dusty miller, and tansy with an eye to their color and texture.

When making a wreath such as this, one or two substitute materials would give you an effect that could be totally different, and that is where the creative excitement comes in: you are in charge, you select the materials, and you bring the design to life with your placement and organization of the elements.

rowing sunflowers has a double reward. The pleasure they bring while blooming is remarkable and can be repeated if you harvest and dry the flowers. Once the petals have faded, I keep a close watch on mine to see that the heads are not damaged by the late-summer elements or the hungry community of birds, and as soon as the seeds are fully developed I bring the flowers in to dry. The heads hold a lot of moisture, and if they are not dried properly they will mold. I hang them from the ceiling or lay them on screens and make sure there is room for air to circulate around them. If you are lucky enough to have a dry attic you'll find it an excellent place to air-dry sunflowers and almost any other kind of plant you harvest.

I wanted to take advantage of the natural roundness of a sunflower head so I filled the center of this one with moss and let the seeds stand as a wreath around it. I added a few oats and rose hips and hung it on this weathered door, where I particularly liked the textural play of the neatly radiating seeds with the alligatored paint. I think dried sunflowers are wonderful to display outdoors. I find the graphic accent of a big wreath of them on a barn or fence visually appealing, while birds and squirrels are attracted to it for another reason: Sunflowers can be a valuable food source for wildlife. I like to bring a few things back to nature after their season has passed.

To begin a wreath like this, make a hanging loop with a florists'-tape-covered wire; insert it through the center of the sunflower, bring the ends together at the circumference, and twist them together. Using your hot-glue gun, attach a clump of moss to the center of the flower head, and cover the wire with corn husk. To trim the wreath and mask the loop, make a spray of boxwood, aromatic cedar, and about fifteen stems of oats. Tie them together and attach to the loop. Use your hot-glue gun to embellish this spray with small rose hips and some German statice. The materials I chose to work with came either from my garden or local florist; if you make a wreath such as this you might prefer to garnish it with some of the things you have gathered on walks and stored in your workroom.

I have a long-standing love for the complex textures of moss and lichen; they remind me of peaceful walks through the forested areas near my home. When I decided to use them as the basis for this wreath I looked through my studio and discovered a bunch of air-dried golden coxcomb, whose muted color and compact texture seemed completely sympathetic with them.

I wanted the surface of this wreath to have a pattern that might be found in nature, and as I arranged the components I sensed that clustering them would give the effect I was seeking. I felt that a darker material would emphasize this pattern, heightening the rather subtle contrast of the moss, lichen, and flowers, so I added some smallish pinecones to pull the eye in and out of the composition.

If you are a collector of intriguing natural materials you will find it a pleasure to begin your design process with a search through your supplies to see what is on hand and which combinations are inspiring at the moment. Had I made this wreath on another day it might have been quite different. I might have added bits of bark or a few small pods and twigs. Every time I begin a design I approach it with a freshness of thought and take inspiration from the things around me.

he last picking from this year's garden yielded three large kale plants. Their leaves have a wonderful color and contour. I experimented to find the best way to dry them, placing a few leaves on wire racks in my attic and a few in silica gel. I learned that the silica gel–dried leaves lost some of their color while those air-dried in the attic held theirs quite well; these had some curling but I liked that quality as it looked very natural. This was important since I planned to combine the kale with other naturally dried materials.

When you begin a wreath you must decide whether to apply your decorative materials directly to the base or to cover it with another material first. I often prefer the interplay of colors and textures when I introduce a covering; in this case I used Spanish moss. Then, to establish a rhythm of color, I hot-glued the kale leaves onto the moss. Some leaves were grouped, overlapping one another, while others were slightly twisted and glued down singly, spreading the color about the surface in a pleasing cadence.

To create a focal point I added a cluster of pinecones and poppy pods; they add weight and their colors pick up tints from the leaves and moss. The kale leaf is remarkable for the deep, lovely purple of its spine; to accentuate this I added some vivid magenta globe amaranth, and then hid a few deep red roses beneath the leaves to surprise the viewer. To balance these, I used small flower clusters taken from bush-dried hydrangea blossoms, which would have been too massive in their entirety. By cutting apart the hydrangeas I was also able to select the individual florets whose color I felt would work best in the composition.

I find that monochromatic compositions can be fascinating. A single color can have many values and subtle tints that are accentuated by textural differences. By arranging similarly colored materials with care you can create a pattern of more complexity than you might think; in keeping with the color, its mood will be gentle or intense.

This dried flower wreath is covered with a mix of similarly colored but disparately textured components. There are flowers from the rain tree (which grows in Florida and similar environments but is available dried from most florists), straw flowers, small leaves, and artificial berries arranged on a base wrapped with unfurled paper ribbon. The pale pink rain tree flower is a marvelous full cluster of petals; the structure of each blossom is somehow

different from the next, making it an ideal choice for a design that is interesting in its subtle variations. The furrowed paper and darker-toned berries create pockets of shadow, while the rounded flat leaves bounce light onto the rain tree flowers; the rose-colored straw flowers smooth the transition from one tone to the next, and their spiky texture adds a little element of surprise.

I began this wreath with a length of the paper ribbon, which I untwisted and wrapped around a straw base, securing the ends with some hot glue. I wired a few loops of this ribbon into a bow and added it to the wreath. All the other components were wired onto florists' picks so that I could adjust their relative positions as I poked them into the straw—if the surface became too dense the subtlety would be lost.

lthough I most often work in a circular format, many wreath designs can be adapted to the heart shape, where they assume overtones of romance or sweetness. Heart-shaped bases can be purchased in the same materials as the circular ones: vine, straw, wire, and foam. When you compose in this symmetrical form, be particularly aware of the balance and angles between each component. Your design need not *be* symmetrical but it should acknowledge the weight and movement of the base.

This wreath was made by wrapping small bunches of wild rose hips and sea lavender onto a simple wire frame with twine. You could substitute German statice for the sea lavender, or baby's breath would work as well. As ever, begin your wreath by wiring on a hanging loop and then tie the twine securely to the point of the heart so that you will be able to put some tension on it as you work. Place a small cluster of statice on the wire, stems toward the notch, and wrap a few times with the twine. Add another small cluster over the stems of the first, placing it at a slightly different angle and wrap again—you will see that you cannot wrap "under" the stems already in place but must always place the next cluster on top of the previous one. Proceeding so that the "blossom" end of your material always faces in roughly the same direction, continue around the frame in this manner, varying the statice with rose hips as you wish and adjusting the angle of the stems so that the heart shape is well filled out. Once you have ended the wrapping you may need to add a few additional sprigs to the notch or point so they are graceful. You can do this with the hot-glue gun if it is difficult to wrap them on between the materials already in place.

I like to use small wreaths to capture the essence of each season. A smaller wreath provides a natural base for delicately scaled elements that could be lost or overshadowed on a large one. Also it can be displayed in so many more places. You can tuck a little wreath into a bookcase or a stairwell cranny, or hang one over a kitchen cupboard or bedpost. A small wreath can simply lie on a coffee table, or on the table beside your favorite chair.

Small wreaths are quick and easy to assemble, so you can turn to them when you need a thoughtful, personal gift. I always feel that once I have the materials assembled I should make two. A number of friends who once lived in my part of the country but have since moved welcome these little wreaths as reminders of seasons they no longer experience.

This small autumn wreath was constructed on a purchased foam base that I covered with Spanish moss. Dividing it (by eye) into six segments, I attached the base of an open pinecone to each with hot glue, and framed each cone with a ring of six hazelnuts. I accented this repeating motif with lines of small pinecones that had been rubbed with white paint, which helped them blend with the colors of the moss. By choosing this color contrast for the smaller pinecones I was able to fill in the open spaces between the clusters in a way that was both orderly and interesting.

To hang this wreath I selected a beautiful ombré ribbon that picked up the shades of the cones, nuts, and moss. Once I had hung the wreath over the mirror I added a graceful stem of bittersweet, bringing a touch of warmth to the glass and to the subtle muted browns of the composition.

Three simple candle collars, each one brownish, made from pinecones or nuts, and each designed to ring a pillar candle. After I make such a statement I ask myself, Why couldn't they be made in a smaller scale and used with candlesticks? I feel it is very important to continually question yourself—as well as the work you do—for there is rarely a reason why you cannot enlarge or reduce a design to work in diverse circumstances. Specific materials might need to be reconsidered, but the concept will very often survive.

The wreaths were constructed on purchased bases to which pinecones or nuts were individually hot-glued or wired. I used a double-wire form for the larger pinecone wreath on the left; I twisted florists' wire through each pinecone and then secured it to the base. I began the arrangement at the perimeter with a ring of nearly identical pinecones; as I added rings toward the center I varied the cones and dotted one ring with acorns. I consid-

ered burnishing the edges of the cones with a copper spray to add a little glimmer to their somber tones, but I enjoy the natural shading and felt that by leaving it I could use the wreath throughout the year.

I made the small wreath in the center by gluing tiny hemlock cones to a small grass wreath I had found in a craft store. Again I worked toward the center to arrange the cones, setting them at various angles so that the candlelight would play across the surface and be caught in interesting patterns.

Diagonal bands of hazelnuts glued across a small moss-covered form create a very different pattern on the third candle collar, where they seem to twine through the center, wrapping the wreath. There are any number of small garnishes you might choose instead of hazelnuts to create a similar garland effect: bands of red and white pistachio nuts, tiny dried roses or other small flowers, shells—anything small and repetitive that pleases you.

ature has certainly provided us with an extraordinary array of pinecones. They can be as tiny as my thumbnail or bigger than my hand and come in many shapes and textures. Wonderfully, no two ever seem to be exactly alike so there is always a chance to find the one that perfectly fills a space or provides the desired gesture. I find it is always a treat to visit my local florist at Christmas, when the display of pinecones is extensive; some are familiar and local while others are exotic and come from faraway places. I never fail to pick up a few of the more unusual ones for the unknown moments when they will add just the right shape or texture to a composition. I find that I use pinecones throughout the year, as they can complement a range of diverse elements. There are also many different surface treatments you can apply to them—paint, dye, metallics—and sometimes I cut the long tubular cones in half lengthwise to expose the pale vein that runs through the center of the dark scales.

In designing the crescent-shaped embellishment for this grapevine wreath I used a variety of pinecones, each selected for its contrast *and* compatibility with the next. As I composed this arrangement I concentrated on the overall texture and surface rhythm while acknowledging the individuality of each piece. Despite the fact that my vocabulary was limited to the pinecones, the design is one of interesting contrast and distinctive gesture.

here are times when a particular material will serve as the inspiration for a design. I will see something intriguing in a shape or texture and challenge myself to use it to advantage. I begin by gathering up a quantity of the material in question, and exploring its potential by arranging it, manipulating it, and juxtaposing it with other things; as I do this I am constantly observing the variations that occur, selecting those that are interesting and pleasing, eliminating those that do not work.

One year I collected some magnolia leaves as they were about to fall and put them in the attic to air-dry. I was immediately intrigued by the variations within this group of like elements and arranged them in an overlapping manner; I found that the independently curling ends and rippling sides flowed around the wreath and their energy intensified the pattern that emerged.

On the top of the wreath I arranged a cluster of dried pomegranates, lemons, deep magenta coxcomb, and small tansy blossoms. To help the design flow into the lower part of the wreath, I let the colorful elements wander into a swag of pinecones that in turn moves into the leaves. Because the leaves have their own energy and texture they are enhanced rather than overwhelmed by the fruit and flowers. By the way, it is possible to buy preserved magnolia leaves, which come flat and dyed a deep green. Though they work well in some situations, I think their effect would be too regimental for this design, with its rich, contrasting palette and shifting textures. Here the seemingly disparate elements all contribute to the rhythmic flow of the composition. When you combine elements and mix them up in ways that are unusual but pleasing you really take control of the creative process.

utumn's palette is not always bronzed and rusted. There are many late-blooming blue and pink flowers that dry gracefully, in beautiful shades and hues. They are lovely massed together in gentle homage to summer's fading glories.

Here a wonderful mass of larkspur, globe amaranth, hydrangea, straw flowers, statice, and wild rose hips covers a straw ring, the soft hues fading in and out of one another in a swathe of pink and mauve. These flowers are so different that it is easy to be aware of the diversity of scale and texture as you balance them around the wreath, setting round full blossoms against long spurs and delicate sprays so that all dimensions are soft and very free. Notice that the deeper-toned flowers and leaves help to draw the eye into the wreath, anchoring the overflowing arrangement—without them it would seem to fall off the base.

In principle, this wreath does not differ dramatically from the previous one—the surface is full, loose, and anchored with darker-toned foliage—but the palette is more limited and the components fewer. I chose hydrangea as the principal flower; it is very delicate, with many shades of soft green and pink on each blossom head, and its compact texture makes a naturally overblown base for the design. I emphasized the subtle beauty of this single flower with sprays of German statice, oak leaves, and some

bunny tail grass, weaving a French ribbon into the arrangement as I worked.

You may find that hydrangea is brittle and difficult to work with. To overcome this, place the blooms in your bathroom and let them absorb some steam from a hot shower, or hold them over a steaming kettle. Remove them as soon as they become pliable; if they get too soft they will not return to their attractive dried state. Often I wet German statice under the faucet, which immediately softens it and makes it easier to use.

Very often the structural support of a wreath can be hidden under all the materials that make up the design. Here I took a foam base and covered it with freshly gathered moss, effectively erasing the base from view. I assembled a lavish assortment of flowers and arranged them around the center of this mossy ring so that the bright garland is wreathed in soft green. I set the other elements on the moss without attaching them and experimented with different effects. Alternating warm and cool colors, interspersing them with some white and silvery ones, gave a charming summery design. I began with some randomly placed preserved galax leaves and then put in the pomegranates and pinecones. To these I added the dried flowers, roughly alternating red and yellow straw flowers with blue thistles and statice and balancing them with white blossoms. I had a lovely but even, low, dense arrangement. A few sprigs of wild rose hips and eucalyptus berries, which dance lightly above the massed flowers, added that unexpected bloom or shape you might encounter in nature, springing seemingly from nowhere. A small touch, but one that I think meets my challenge.

moss over the straw and wrapped it in place with florist twine. This process is simple and I often use it to save time; the ornamental materials I use always cover the mechanics. In addition, since no glue is involved, the base can be reused easily.

Once covered with moss, the wreath was ready for the flowers. My scheme here was flexible, with an assortment of different materials to unify. I had color changes and textural variations to consider as well as differences in scale, and I wanted the rhythm of the arrangement to be fluid rather than static. I like to take a spontaneous, almost impulsive approach to wreath making and sometimes let the materials control the design. It is good to see a few chance relationships emerge from within the overall scheme of things.

One of the great charms of the French ribbon suspending this wreath is the thin wire along each edge that holds whatever position you give it. You can curl, crumple, and adjust it as you wish to determine the specific character of its gesture. Happily, it comes in the most spectacular assortment of colors and patterns. Here a relatively long loop of it was threaded through the wreath and between the flowers, then knotted at the top, where it hangs over a hook. The bow was made separately and caught to the top of the loop with a few stitches (a pin would work as well). The tails hang free; their characteristic gesture made possible by the wire. I encourage you to experiment with French ribbon, you will appreciate its expressive potential.

H ere a harvest wreath, hung on a bedroom door with a formal French ribbon bow, is a pretty expression of autumn. Dried globe thistle, pepper berries, German statice, and straw flowers were arranged in an allover pattern. Though it lacks a tight symmetrical order, this wreath maintains its strong sense of organization because the weight of the colors is balanced over the surface.

This wreath was constructed on a straw base that had been covered with Spanish moss. I laid the

Silica drying is one of the best ways to retain the beauty of flowers grown in your garden, purchased at a farmer's market, or received as a gift. Drying and preserving a good supply of flowers yourself assures that you will be able to work with exceptional blooms long out of season. I have plastic sweater boxes that I keep my flowers in, much like the museum curator who has drawers of specimens. As I am creating a wreath I will go through these boxes to discover just the right flower to bring an element of surprise to the design, as I did when making this zinnia wreath.

I had dried the last of my zinnias with a mind toward making a winter wreath of summer flowers; when I began it I found that I wanted a different scale and a contrasting texture to play against the sharp petal form of the dominating flower. Discovering the small but bright black-eyed Susans and the soft-petaled roses in my stash of silica-dried flowers answered both of these concerns, and allowed me to enhance the character of my design.

I first covered a straw ring with moss that I had gathered on a mountain walk. As soon as I began to establish the rhythm and color of the zinnia arrangement I knew I wanted to leave some of the moss exposed. The proportion of background that peeks through a composition can be influenced by the color scheme or ultimate place of display, as well as the nature of the covering itself. If you work on a background of lichen or moss, or any other material that creates a rich or subtle surface, you immediately challenge the elements that you place upon it. I find this challenge healthy, and it keeps my designing free from repetitive habits.

The zinnias were glued to the moss one at a time in loose clusters so that the colors drift, carrying the eye around the wreath. The smaller flowers were then worked among the larger ones, and the contrasting petal texture of the rose created the tension that I had wanted to establish. I wanted this to be a calm wreath, but with a punch.

recognized the potential of this unusual base the first time I saw it at my florist's. The shape is fully dimensional and its open construction is a remarkable example of weaving. When I brought it to my studio I thought its strong character would be best left unadorned, but later I began to feel that some embellishment would invite the eye to travel in as well as around the ring. I decided to enhance it with a variety of dried (and mostly curvilinear) materials, which I arranged with regard to their relative size, color, and scale.

Some of the specific elements I used had to be purchased, but a similar wreath of mixed naturals could be created from things gleaned from the woods or your landscape. When you make an arrangement like this you can often find a place for oddments left over from other projects, or for a singular element that had never found the right home. The establishment of compositional harmony is most important; the way in which you juxtapose one shape or color against another should challenge your creativity. I feel that a composition of this nature offers the designer a chance to push beyond the familiar.

When I began this wreath I took moss gathered from my yard and hot-glued it to the back at random intervals, setting color into the form and reinforcing its third dimension. Then I wove lengths of curly willow into the open structure to enliven the surface and break up the rigidity.

I chose to focus the embellishment with two very large air-dried artichokes that had opened slightly and turned a wonderful color. I anchored these to the wreath with hot glue, reinforcing the bonds with moss—this is a good trick when gluing something heavy to an open base. I connected the artichokes with rhythmic sweeps of cecropia leaves that reiterate but are not confined by the movement in the woven wreath. Next I added the dark lotus pods and pinecones, and worked the mushrooms in against their shapes and colors.

Some time before, I had received a package of dried materials from Florida and in it were a few long pale green pods. Their muted color and punctuated texture appealed to me but I had never found the right place to use them. Here, their shape was a foil to the many curves and I liked the way they brought the deeper green tones of the moss to the front. Finally, the monochromatic composition wanted a staccato punch, so I accented with a few sprigs of bittersweet and red berries.

A wreath, like a painting, can tell a story. Perhaps an epic is not possible, but surely a small essay, a memory, or a reflection of some importance to the creator, of some pleasure to the viewer, can be stated in such a confined space? Here, then, is a garden narrative. A tale of youthful ramblings behind my father's greenhouses. A story of the treasures I found discarded and the gifts of nature that grew, by design or otherwise, outside those well-tended structures.

I began this story with an oval straw base. I covered it with clumps of lichen and green and Spanish moss, intending that these would give me a background of contrasting colors and textures. I remember vividly the terracotta that was everywhere around the greenhouse, so I looked through my potting shed and found two small pots and a few shards. The pots I filled with blocks of foam

and then planted with miniature dried roses; I placed them toward the center of the oval, where they are the focus of this composition. The shards set around the wreath look just like those I used to find behind the greenhouse. Remembering the way small flowers always grew among them, I placed some stray petals and few small roses in the moss as if the wind had planted them there. I nestled raffia-bound sprigs of lavender among the pottery, letting them break the circumference of the oval, and added air-dried kale and blue thistle so that the purply-blue color would contrast the green all around my design. I am always intrigued by the way subtle variations of one color, in this case the purple tones of the kale, thistle, and lavender, echo around a composition. The poppy pods at the bottom of the wreath balance the light gray lichen at the top, pulling the eye through the center.

When picking sage to bring into my kitchen for winter, the scent from its leaves inspired me to begin a wreath. I went into my studio and found a Styrofoam ring that I had covered with Spanish moss, as I often do in anticipation of a time when a background of Spanish or green moss—or even lichen—will enhance other materials. I wired bunches of three or four sprigs of sage onto florists' picks that I poked into the center and outer edges of the wreath. I knew the sage would eventually dry and curl, a characteristic I took into account as I added the subsequent materials. I next inserted golden oats, allowing just enough space between each bunch of three for straw flowers.

At this point the wreath was predominantly silver-gray with cream accents, and I added a few sprigs of tansy for contrast. Feeling that the composition needed the balance of a subtle, deep green, I tucked in some air-dried galax leaves, which have a wonderful lifelike gesture.

Later, after the sage leaves had dried, I added sprigs of lavender foliage, which has a short leaf that holds its shape and is a good filler. It also keeps its silver-green color when dry and so sustained the existing color harmony.

A small wreath of freshly picked herbs makes a charming gift, something to cook from, to adorn a friend's kitchen. Giving such a wreath lets you express your creativity in a thoughtful way.

This is a very simple wreath to assemble and the scent that wafts from the herbs rewards every step. Begin with a small straw base and some twine—you can use the ordinary kitchen twine that one always has on hand, or even raffia—I used florists' twine, as I wanted it to disappear against the herbs. Choose any woody-stemmed herbs you fancy—you might like to use an assortment or just one kind— select them for their flavor, scent, color, or texture as you wish. (I mixed a bit of dusty miller in with my herbs because I like the way its soft gray works with their soft green.) Cluster the herbs into bunches and lay them over the straw base in a way that pleases you and simply wrap them with the twine.

I decided this wreath would be enhanced with the addition of contrasting color and texture, so I added some lady apples and a few leaves and fruits snipped from my calamondin tree. The brightly colored fruits glow like little gems against the greenery, and the sharp leaves shine among the herbs like signposts pointing around the wreath.

If you plan your herb wreath as a gift consider further embellishments: you could label the herbs on old-fashioned tags. Or think of tying on some herb seed packets so that your friend can replenish the wreath. A design concept is like a seed; it will grow if you nourish it with creativity.

eed pods always seem so exotic, interesting, and unusual to me. This is because they are often from lands beyond our reach, and their odd forms invoke a sense of mystery. I enjoy the textures of pods, the way they grow, the manner in which they dry. Their color—or lack of it—appeals to me as does the way they complement other, more familiar forms. The pods used on this wreath represent foreign lands and many unknowns; each was chosen for its individual character and unique shape.

Because pods are durable and can withstand the elements, they work equally well in wreaths made for interior display or those specially designed to grace the out-of-doors. Use them with other naturals—fruits and berries, seasonal vines, and other assorted materials you pick from your own landscape. Leave their surface as you found it, as I did here, or coat them with varnish to give them a subtle sheen. (Sometimes at holidays I spray them lightly with gold or silver to liven up a composition.) Pods are widely available through craft supply or florist's shops, or you may discover some that are new and interesting when you travel; if so, pick them up and take them back to your studio for use at a later time.

Here I combined dried lotus and poppy pods with others that came from my florist, and arranged them with mushrooms, galax leaves, thistles, and artichokes on a foam base that had been covered with gray Spanish moss. The arrangement is not symmetrical but the elements are balanced. As I positioned the pods I considered the subtle colors, textures, and visual weight of each, as well as their gestures. I felt it was essential to give the composition a tight, interesting rhythm with energy that played against itself.

Initially, my materials were selected for the closeness of their color and disparity of size. I had intended to hold the palette to a monochromatic beige-brown, but as I worked I felt the need to include a muted green and chose air-dried galax leaves, since their naturally curled and buckled edges would complement all the odd pod shapes.

Constructing this wreath was fairly simple. Many of the pods had strong natural stems, which I wired onto three-inch (7.5-cm) florists' picks. Those that were without stems I simply hot-glued in place. Always consider the weight of your materials when attaching them with hot glue: If you are attaching a heavy object, make sure it has two points of contact with the base, and hold it until the bond feels secure, for if it falls the glue could burn you.

The place in which you display your wreath can affect the success of its composition as much as any of the other design principles with which you work. If you know where you will be hanging a specific piece there are a number of things to consider before beginning. What is the size of the space and how should you scale your wreath to be most effec-

tive in it? What are the other objects in the space and which textures and colors will best complement them? Should you make a piece that is active or sedate? I find that when you are able to consider these matters up front the wreath will be particularly successful, the design integrated creatively with the space.

In this corner of my library I had very deliberately set up a vignette with the sculptural pieces on the desk below the frames on the wall. I knew that I wanted something soft to contrast them that would pull the eye from one area to the other. I chose to make a small wreath of dried materials that would share some of the colors in this environment, and have both curved and linear elements. Hanging in this space, it creates a tension between the arm of the African sculpture and the handle of the pitcher while it anchors the corners of the frames. There is movement between all these objects. A large wreath would not have worked here, it would have been too heavy. Something smaller than this would have been insignificant among the other very graphic objects. Anything dimensional takes on a life of its own and must coexist with the other things in its vicinity. If you can plan for this before you begin you will not be frustrated in the end by a concept that is inherently out of place.

lthough a wreath is often circular in form, I don't see any reason why it must always be based upon a coil or dough-nut shape and a continuous and sinu-ous circumference. Every now and then I like to take a linear material and arrange it into a curvili-near shape without actually bending it. This can result in an energetic composition that is direct, simple, and apparently spontaneous.

Here I wrapped an assortment of twigs and heather stems onto a wire ring with florists' twine, which I then masked with an embellishment of straw flowers, globe thistle and statice. This is really one of the simplest of wreaths to make. Begin by wiring a hanging loop onto the ring, then tie the twine on securely near it. Wrap a small cluster of twigs onto the ring with the twine. Place another cluster next to the first, overlapping slightly if appropriate, and wrap again. As you continue around the ring add in a few stems of heather if you wish—I like the contrast of its soft, delicate texture against the stark and brittle twigs. You may find that an excess of stems is building up toward the center of the ring; simply cut them with pruners, tapering them to echo the round form of the ring.

Once you have completed the twig circle and tied off the twine, arrange the flowers as you like and secure them with hot glue. Because the twigs and heather surrounded this wreath with such a sense of abandon I chose to impose a bit of order on the flowers, spacing them evenly around the ring and alternating light with dark colors.

Since this type of wreath is so easy to assemble you might like to take the basic supplies—wire ring, twine, and pruners—with you on a hike through

the countryside. Who knows what wonderful mate-rials you might encounter as you amble? A day in the open, spent gathering and making wreaths, will be one of healthy and creative exercise that remains a favored memory.

I always try to make designs that are not static, that have movement and surprise. Because wreaths are usually circular there is some activity inherent to their observation—the eye must travel around to see the detail—but it is possible to use color, texture, and shape to create an illusion of movement strong enough to actually pull the viewer around the surface.

By choosing to superimpose diagonal swathes of sea-foam colors across the ring shape of the base I have made it appear that this wreath is wrapped with ropes of moss. The movement is intensified by the textural variations of the materials but unified by the limited palette. In truth, the only element that actually wraps through the ring is a multiple strand of dyed green reed; it emphasizes the movement as it sails lightly over the surface and culminates in the cluster of pods and reeds that seems to explode off one edge of the composition.

This illusion of natural energy was actually carefully planned and arranged. I first completely covered a straw base with green moss so that I would be free to establish the design without having to worry about the structural support peeking through. I chose teal and sea green gypsophila (baby's breath) and wired small clusters of each onto three-inch

(7.5-cm) florists' picks. I "draped" the gyp in widely spaced diagonal bands over the wreath (securing it with the picks) and then paralleled it with bands of teal. I wired each end of the dyed reed onto picks, secured one as an anchor, and wrapped the other through the wreath, following the pattern of the gypsophila. I then added some sprigs of light green springerii (a fernlike green) to round out the effect.

I used all sorts of materials in the cluster that secures the ends of the wrapped swag—artichokes, poppy pods, black beard wheat, mushrooms, thistle, galax leaves, artificial berries, and long reed stems—choosing them for their round or linear shape and blue-green or wheat coloration (or, as with the dried artichokes, brushing them with verdigris paint if their color was not in this palette.) As I arranged the pods and reeds I tried to echo the circular sweep of the wreath but at the same time to break free of its confines, letting the variations of shape and color lead the eye in a game of dimensional hide-and-seek.

The center of a wreath need not be empty, and when I am designing I often think of ways to use the circle to enclose and set off some other element. This concept works very logically when the wreath lies on a table, where it can hold candles, fruit, or whatever. Turn this idea and think of a hanging wreath as a frame for something other than the wall that supports it.

Here a floral wreath surrounds a mirror, where it frames the face of anyone who gazes into it. This idea of encircling the head with flowers is delightful—a flower-trimmed looking glass would be a nice detail in a guest room or bath, or might open the land of dreams for any young girl whose wall it adorned.

I made this wreath from a melange of dried flowers, arranging them so that the colors flow around the ring and using the different shapes and densities in a lighthearted way. When you design a mirror-frame wreath you suddenly have a new dimension to consider. The glass reflects everything that is before it—this naturally includes any materials used on the frame that wander into the center—

and the "picture" alters as the viewer varies his position. As you make your arrangement you must be constantly aware of how it looks reflected in the glass and be sure that the mechanics of construction are neat or hidden. You may find that the balance of the composition does not work as you expect; the reflection may make the center elements appear heavier or more intense than those at the circumference. Magically. This reflective quality may work to your advantage; you are able to show more than one view of your materials and capture color and movement in unexpected ways.

You can purchase mirrors already framed by foam rings of several sizes at craft supply stores and florists, which solves the logistical problem of how to get the mirror attached to the wreath, and leaves you free to develop the design as you wish. Before beginning, check to make sure there is a way to hang the mirror and add a wire if necessary. The foam ring is very convenient and easy to work with; you can either insert the stems of your materials right into it, or glue them on, as you prefer. Of course, you can use a wood frame but you will have to glue the elements of the wreath to it.

CHAPTER
2

WREATHS FOR
SPECIAL OCCASIONS

or many people Christmas is a holiday suffused with traditions. I think there is no other time of year so marked by festive display and a mood of joy, wonder, and excitement. There are as many ways to decorate for Christmas as there are people to celebrate the day, but there are certain conventions that convey the mood of the season year after year—themes, colors, smells, symbols—and I find these endlessly inspiring and always evocative. The images of snow, greenery, candlelight, swathes of brilliant red, gold, silver, the aromas of holiday baking, of pine and balsam, strains of age-old song—I am enriched by it all.

The most traditional Christmas wreaths are made of evergreens and trimmed with red, and I never tire of them. Within the world of evergreens and red there are infinite possibilities and I see new ones every season. This wreath, for instance, is made of fragrant juniper and dusted with tiny white flowers as though caught in a light snowfall; vibrant red tulips replace the expected bow.

I am drawn to juniper, with its sculptural foliage and waxy blue-green berries that fill the air with their lovely scent. However, I know that the birds love the berries as much as I do, so I tend to use juniper for very special occasions only. Here I wired small branches of it together and wrapped the resulting wreath loosely with a lovely deep green French ribbon. I put the tulips and star of Bethlehem in water picks before placing them in the juniper, and then tucked in the baby's breath. Juniper is a wonderfully textured evergreen; the baby's breath echoes that texture while the tulip petals and taffeta ribbon contrast it. The fresh flowers give this design special elegance (they will last in the water picks for a day or two—certainly long enough to grace a family gathering or a festive dinner), but the wreath of juniper, with its pretty berries, dusting of tiny white flowers, and meander of ribbon, would still be lovely if the tulips fade and must be removed.

Instead of choosing the usual pine boughs for the background of this wreath I used fresh laurel, which has interesting clusters of leaves. I cut short stems of the laurel and simply poked them into a foam ring, giving it a wonderful dense, rich green covering. I sprayed a few of the clusters copper, and when they dried I placed them somewhat randomly around the wreath. Continuing this theme, I tucked metallic ribbon–covered balls (in copper and two shades of blue) in among the laurel leaves, where they shimmer through the dense foliage like exotic animals in a jungle, contributing weight and accent to the pattern. The graceful, airy copper gauze ribbon bow catches the eye without being too heavy, and helps it travel around the wreath. The asymmetrical pattern and the off-center placement of the bow were completely intentional. By gently shifting the focal elements to the left I was able to avoid the expected design, just as I had avoided the expected material.

Why not try out a number of holiday compositions using laurel as an alternative background? It is also lovely in combination with other greens and naturals. The important thing is to experiment, to try out as many combinations as you can imagine. This process of experimental discovery is in itself one of the most beautiful and satisfying aspects of creative work.

Discovering this assortment of Mexican ornaments inspired me to make a narrative wreath of the Christmas story. The tin ornaments are new; to bring out the relief details that tend to disappear on this shiny surface I toned them with paint. Knowing

that I planned to use dried yellow roses and calamondin oranges in the design, I decided to give the ornaments an ochre cast: First I painted them with deep green acrylic, when it was just dry I rubbed most of it off with a damp sponge. I let the ornaments dry completely and then repeated this process with ochre acrylic paint.

The ornaments have a charming naif quality. I felt they would tell their story best in a symmetrical manner so I arranged them freehand to mirror-image on the boxwood background. (I used hot glue to attach the ornaments to florists' picks— eight inches (20cm) long for the large ornaments, three inches (7.5cm) long for the small ones.) The two larger angels hold the wreath between them, calling attention to the star that shines over the tale of wonder. I placed the smaller ornaments on the wreath in a cascading pattern flowing to and from the center, setting the fruits, roses, and little gold pinecones in counterpoint to them. The concentration of activity above the little church serves to balance the design, assuring that the eye is drawn down from the large angels at the top.

There are many ways to develop a creative concept. You might take the same one and bring to it your own sense of proportion, your own quality of design. You should always remember that you, the designer, can choose the way you want your work to look. If you wonder what I mean, stop for a moment to think how many times the Christmas story has been told in how many ways.

Each of the year's holidays has its traditional accoutrements, those decorative embellishments that seem absolutely festive when in season and rather odd when not. At Christmas red-and-white peppermint candies seem unquestionably essential so I decided to use them in combination with some fresh holly to make a not-too-serious but very graphic wreath.

This wreath was a very simple one to construct. The two materials contrast one another sharply and divide the wreath in half. I began with a foam base and added a wire loop through which I could later thread a ribbon for hanging. Then I wired small clusters of fresh holly and berries to florists' picks and covered the top half of the ring with them, keeping the individual clusters as natural looking as I could so that the surface and edge would be lively and interesting.

I wired individually wrapped peppermints to florists' picks in groups of three (wrap the wire around the cellophane twists). I covered the lower half of the wreath with these, varying the angle of insertion so they would appear as full and spontaneous as the holly above. I stuck a bit of holly in among the peppermints to bring some green into the red and white, just as the variegated leaves and bright berries carry some red and white up into the green. To mask the hard lines dividing the halves I tied on two generous red satin bows and set them at jaunty angles. Visually, their weight anchors the composition and saves it from being trite.

I can think of many ways to play with the juxtaposition of holiday candies and greens. First of all, there are many sorts of brightly wrapped candies to choose from or combine. You could place them in stripes across the green or in blocks that quarter the wreath. Mix up all the elements and scatter them around the wreath like confetti. Let your imagination go and have fun with the variations.

though nature does a wonderful job of year-round decorating we all seem to feel a need to give her a hand near our homes. We plant lawns and cultivate gardens, we feel that architecture without landscaping is somehow incomplete, yet architecture adorned by the free hand of nature is not something most of us want to live with.

At holiday time, particularly in climates where winter makes the landscape stark or bleak, outdoor decorations serve as a reminder to friends and passersby that it is the season of festivity. I like outdoor decorations that pay homage to their setting, that acknowledge the proximity of nature, so when I design them I look to see what the landscape is like and use it as my inspiration.

This classic country barn is plain, simple, and straightforward; to be in the holiday mood it needed just a simple, classic wreath, but one with the spirit of its country setting. A wreath of mixed

winter greens and pinecones looks perfectly natural against the gray boards, the soft ribbon flows freely in the winter breeze, and the little red cardinals might just have perched there to shelter from the snow (I must admit they came via the florist).

I covered a straw wreath with Spanish moss so that I would have a unified green ground on which to compose. I cut some branches from nearby greenery and just laid them over the moss-covered form, securing them with wire when I liked the way they looked. By placing each branch individually, I was able to control the line of the wreath, to establish the cascading movement of the greens against the deep background of moss. Once I had this basic arrangement in place I filled it in and gave it more dimension with bits of greenery wired to florists' picks. The pinecones and pepper berries, also attached to picks, nod out of the greens much as they would if growing there. The red ribbon, birds, and berries complement the greenery.

I strongly believe that one should look to nature for inspiration. There are times when the character of a particular flower is so distinctive that it can stand alone. Sometimes the only designing one need do is to recognize the beauty and possibility of the material, and then intensify what one sees.

In the fall I took a number of rich, velvety coxcomb from my garden and hung them upside down in my attic. They dried quite quickly in the warmth up under the eaves and when I cut them down I spent a few moments admiring their lush color and incredible, convoluted texture. I decided to make a coxcomb wreath—a continuous oval of undulating, velvety saturated color.

Once dry the coxcomb breaks apart into small, sturdy components that are easy to handle. I used hot glue to secure them to the oval form, trying to recreate that wonderful rippled surface that characterizes this majestic flower. When you make an entire wreath of just one material you create a very graphic form. In this case the wreath was luxurious as well, and I felt that it warranted an equally opulent flourish, so I twisted a tassel-trimmed upholstery cord through the center. Depending upon the style of your home, you might prefer the wreath unadorned, particularly once the holiday is past.

There are many ways you can interpret this single-element wreath concept and several examples are shown in this book. Working with just one color and texture allows you a simplicity and clarity that is very direct. If the material is beautiful in itself and you find the right shape and proportion in which to display it, it will not be boring.

A traditional balsam wreath tied with a bright red bow heralds the winter season in simple, classic style. It is no less festive for all its familiarity—and is appropriate with any architectural style. Perhaps, as I do, you have a neighbor who makes these fragrant wreaths for friends every year. If not, they are readily available at Christmas tree lots. Balsam wreaths are so lovely that I don't think one need ever feel that it might be cheating to simply buy one.

I often bring one or two fresh balsam wreaths into my home for the holidays. The pine scent adds such a lovely fragrance to the tightly closed winter house, infusing it with crisp fresh air. I have friends who keep their balsam wreath all year and enjoy it as it turns a rich, coppery brown. Cut balsam retains both its fragrance and needles as it dries, which is true for some, but not all evergreens.

Designing variations on a theme is always a lot of fun. Give yourself a few parameters, make a wonderful arrangement, and then alter it in some simple way expressing another mood, and you will begin to understand the delightful freedom given by flexibility. When you recognize each variation as a fresh creation that stands on its own, your understanding of design and your creativity grows in a most rewarding way.

To understand the way variables affect mood I set myself an exercise: I wanted to make two very different designs in which some important elements were the same. I decided to explore the potential of a vine wreath that I sprayed gold, some pinecones (also dusted with gold spray), and a gold rope cord. Because it was so tightly wrapped and densely painted, I felt that the wreath was in itself a visually heavy form; the challenge was to free it, lighten it—to embellish it in such a way that it assumed a spirited energy.

I began by tying the gold cord in a bow at the top of the wreath and knotting its ends to hang over the opposite side. I found a marvelous pleated gold ribbon that I twisted and turned around the wreath, weaving the ends into the vine while allowing the ribbon to float rhythmically over the surface. As I arranged the pinecones I thought they

might be complemented by the addition of some dried artichokes. I sprayed these solid gold, and then decided to make the smaller pinecones solid gold as well. I picked some variegated holly and then wired the final arrangement together. Everything seems loose and free, with each element retaining its individuality; the variegated leaves play off the natural color peeking through the lightly dusted cones, the different gold objects give the composition a needed third dimension, and the pleated ribbon and lively sprigs of holly dance freely around it. I had met the first half of my challenge to my satisfaction.

I liked the combination of the green leaves with the gold and decided to intensify this contrast in my variation; I wanted to see if I could use color to make the wreath rich without making the composition heavy. I replaced the pleated gold gauze with streamers of deep green French ribbon. Then I removed the artichokes and some of the holly and introduced a few natural pinecones. I liked what was beginning to happen, but saw that I needed some lighter and brighter color, as well as something to replace the dimension of the artichokes. A few beautiful pieces of fruit met both needs. The wreath had assumed a new character and it was still full of lively movement.

Of course, thematic variations are intriguing in an intellectual sort of way, and you might really think about working with them whenever you must make multiples of one design—for instance when you decorate a large room or church for a holiday or wedding. Often a unified variety of designs is more interesting for both the maker and viewer than a straightforward repetition.

Time evaporates during the holiday season. I'm always running out of it, and I expect everyone else is as well. Sometimes there is just no more energy or money for another creative project, and that's when ingenuity takes over. Some wreaths take quite a bit of time to develop, gather supplies for, and put together, but it is absolutely possible to zip one together if you have a vine wreath and some bits of seasonal greens and ribbon on hand.

I made this holiday wreath very quickly by inserting the cut ends of some greens into the twists of a cranberry-painted vine form. I simply let the materials talk to me—often an honest look at their forms will answer any design questions; they'll remind you that it is best to simply acknowledge their natural characteristics. The colors of nature almost always work together, so I let the different greens of the holly, cedar, and eucalyptus berries fall as they would, bouncing the light off their disparate surfaces. I tied a generous length of French ribbon into a simple bow and let the ends trail freely through the wreath and down the clock case. And before the clock struck and the guests arrived, the room was filled with the fragrance of the greens—this is one of those projects where a great deal of pleasure comes from pulling something so lovely together in no time at all.

ust as the coxcomb holiday wreath on page 67 is made entirely from one flower, this small wreath is made solely from pepper berries. Where the coxcomb wreath pushes the richness of its surface into an oval shape, this wreath is simply round; where the coxcomb surface is deep and mysterious, the pepper berries seem to dance around the form. Here your eye senses no weight, the piece is light as air. It is also rather petite, so it can be hung amid architectural details or favorite sculpture or artwork, or be laid on a table and used to ring a candle. Pepper berries are very long lasting, and a small wreath of them makes a lovely gift.

When I make a wreath from just one material I am very aware of its sculptural qualities; I look at it as an abstract, graphic form with a subtle message to be seen in slight variations of texture and color. There is much less to think about than with a more complicated design, so my appreciation is direct and immediate. When I add another element to such a plain piece the clarity of the design changes, it loses some of its abstract quality and becomes more decorative. This process of effecting change is one of the most fascinating things about design; there is always something new to discover.

lace just one decorative element on a simple wreath and you will change its mood. Here is the same little pepperberry ring with its dancing pink-and-red surface, but I have added a soft loopy bow, set off by a few green leaves. The wreath became sweeter. This ribbon doesn't really tame or control the escaping berries, rather it reiterates their spirit and playful look.

My perception of this wreath changed when I had tied on the bow. I no longer saw it as a graphic round. Moved to hang among the kitchenware, the wreath is more casual, yet more festive.

Wreath making should include the unexpected, and sometimes when you begin a design you should abandon familiar concepts and try to come into the process with fresh ideas. Perhaps you will shift the usual scale of your wreath, or abandon a base that has become routine. Perhaps you will use a familiar material in an atypical way or make a wreath to display in an unexpected place. For instance, the small scale of these holiday wreaths made them perfect for the necks of antique decanters. When completed, I tilted the wreaths gracefully over the decanters to show them at their festive best.

The wreath on the left was easily constructed from florists' wire and small sprigs of boxwood and fragrant cedar. I held two lengths of wire together and shaped them into a ring that sat loosely over the neck of the decanter, remembering that the fresh greens would increase the wreath's volume. I

added the greenery with additional wire, filling the whole circle. I also wired on some acorns, which I had picked with their stems and some leaves, and sprayed gold once they had dried. (If you find that dried acorns drop from their caps, use hot glue to reattach them.) To give the wreath a punch of color I wrapped a length of ombré ribbon around it and glued pairs of artificial berries to it at intervals. Lastly, I added a few hemlock cones.

The wreath on the right was constructed from three lengths of gold cording twisted together and secured with wire. Where the pieces were joined I added a sprig of aromatic cedar and a cluster of lightly gilded pinecones, acorns, and artificial berries (you could use anything festive of similar scale). Although monochromatic, the small embellishments retain some of their natural color; the cording has depth and texture, which adds richness and finesse to the wreath design.

A t Christmas, shimmering, twinkling light enhances the ambience, adding elegance and heightening the sense of mystery. From the tinsel on the tree to the candlelit glow of the best silver on the sideboard, anything that glitters gives us a momentary sense of magic. Whether the flame is candle or electric, there is no easier way to set it dancing than to place it by a reflective surface, so we turn to lustrous silver and gold trimmings to bounce the holiday lights in all directions, to magnify the magic of the season.

Christmas is a season in which I have no objection to the use of a little artifice. Even when I am working with natural materials, if I think the decorations I am creating would be wonderful with a glimmering surface, I'll give them one.

For centuries artisans have been using metal leaf to enrich objects that are not in themselves precious. Today there are synthetic leafing materials that make it easy and inexpensive to add a lustrous metallic surface to almost anything. When I was thinking about making a wreath to trim a formal holiday sideboard I became intrigued with the idea of using a simple arrangement of leaves—silver leaves—so that candlelight would glimmer not only on the silver serving vessels but on the wall above as well. I wanted a leaf that had an inherent formality, so I chose preserved galax leaves, which are round and nearly flat. Once silver-gilt, they assumed an elegance appropriate to the occasion, so I just overlapped them around a base and embellished them with a few sprays of silver bells tied on with a generous plaid taffeta bow.

uring the winter holidays I enjoy going to the market to look for seasonal produce that could add an interesting variation of scale or texture to a wreath. I especially like to work with small, vibrant lady apples or clusters of miniature oranges. I also love pears, which come in wonderful shapes and colors and look well with the smaller fruit, though they don't keep as well at room temperature and have to be checked from time to time. But at this season there are checklists for almost everything, so keeping an eye on a few pears is not a problem.

When I plan to use the fruit near a lighted candle I sometimes like to roll it in sugar, which adds sparkle to the colors (see page 133). Here I circled a red candle with lush holiday greens that I filled with this "crystallized" fruit, adding a bit of magic to the rich red, blushing gold, and cool chartreuse as they played against the variegated greens of the background.

This wreath began with a straw ring set on a crystal cake stand. Sprigs of boxwood, clusters of variegated holly, and a bit of aromatic cedar were wired onto picks that I stuck into the base in a dense but random pattern. When the sugar on the fruit was hard, I poked each piece onto a pick so that I could position it securely on the wreath. I placed two green apples opposite one another in the greenery and then spaced two golden pears unevenly between them so that the composition was loosely balanced. Next came the red lady apples, which I placed singly or in pairs between the larger fruit, adding a visual spark to the cool greens

and bringing a needed warmth and tension to the composition. I had a few small pinecones sprayed gold and I added six of them to the ring. Finally, I tucked a few dried red roses and three or four softly colored dusty miller leaves into the greens.

When the Christmas holidays roll around it seems that most people make their homes more festive and inviting. It is a time when candles and wreaths come into view, lending rich color to familiar spaces. Doors are opened and friends and neighbors invited to enjoy warmth and hospitality.

Wreaths need not be hung to be used effectively; and they needn't always be sturdily built—especially if you want them to last only a short while. Here a festive wreath is "constructed" on a silver tray, with cranberries and pears, fresh greens, and flowers in concentric rings around a pillar candle. A wreath of this type could be made at any time of the year. Think of weddings, anniversary parties, or simply celebrating the seasons. I'd like one of spring flowers with perhaps small cookies or other sweets around the candle. (If you use your tray to hold edible things, place the candle in a candlestick to protect the food from wax.)

A wreath of this type is extremely simple to make. Begin with an elegant tray or use a lovely platter or a plate with a special edge. Center the candle and fill the space around it with fresh cranberries, allowing the edge of the tray to show—the silver contrasting with the red and green is a beautiful detail. On the cranberries place six perfect pears, selected for their red-gold coloring. Place fresh greens—I used cedar and holly—around the outer edge of the tray. (If your tray is footed the greens will slip under the edge and probably stay in place; if not, simply form them into a rope by connecting them with wire in strategic places and twisting the ends together securely.)

When using fresh flowers insert them in water picks before adding them to the wreath. Here I used fresh yarrow, star of Bethlehem, and baby's breath because they pick up the colors of the candle and pears while contrasting the cranberries and greens, thus unifying the whole in a warmly festive way. It is, of course, possible to make lovely variations on this theme by using other flowers or fruit. Let your imagination roam: fill the center of the tray with small pinecones instead of cranberries; reverse the colors by placing kumquats on the tray and substituting red apples for the pears. You could even line the surface of the tray with small holiday balls and place larger ornaments on them; this would certainly add a festive sparkle to your holiday decorations.

The roses clustered among the greens give this fragrant centerpiece its formal, elegant character. The variegated greenery makes a harmonious background for the pure color of the flowers, which is repeated in the simple tapered candles. I arranged fresh cedar, boxwood, and holly, along with a few sprigs of eucalyptus berries, over a florist's foam ring so that they spilled naturally onto the table, then simply poked them securely into it. The foam is firm enough to support the candles, so I pushed them into it as well, and then poked in the roses. Some lady apples and small golden pears add a bit more holiday color and, as a nod to the good food to come, keep the arrangement from being too serious. If you have a long table you might like to change the shape of this centerpiece a bit, extending it with rectangular blocks of foam that run down the middle of the table. This would allow you to send candlelight and the fragrance of roses to guests not seated right at the center.

With a moist florists' foam ring as a base there is no worry about the greens drying out or the roses wilting before the festivities are over. And while I wouldn't leave the candles burning unattended, they are certainly safe enough for the duration of a meal—much safer than real candles would be on a tree. You can create a similar effect using water picks and a straw or foam base, but you would have to keep a more watchful eye on it to be sure it did not dry out—and you would not have nearly the same flexibility of arrangement.

This little group of bears is showing off a selection of miniature wreaths chosen for a *very* festive occasion—perhaps a child's birthday party, or that of a dedicated bear collector. Miniature wreaths are truly enjoyable to make and they bring a lot of pleasure to the child who receives them. Many materials come in diminutive sizes at craft supply or trimmings shops, as well as party stores and florists, so keep your eye out for clusters of small silk flowers or artificial berries that can be separated, fancy braid that can be cut apart, or even doilies and stickers. All you really need in quantity is imagination, or maybe a burning desire to be silly. Otherwise, a few small treasures, some scissors, and a bit of glue and wire (and some purchased miniature wreath forms, if you like) are all that is required.

Small wreaths belong to the world of childhood, so perhaps a small person you know would like to help, or knows of a doll who has nothing to wear to a party (or maybe is too shy to say she'd like to have one in her size as well?). They do make lovely celebration crowns...and they hold the key to imagination that unlocks the land of wonder.

The bears have a few whimsical suggestions to proffer; you will no doubt have many ideas of your own. For the bear at the upper left, it could be the Fourth of July, with American flags and ripe red cherries (these are actually lacquered miniature apples). I glued them with some white artificial berries to a purchased grapevine wreath and Bear is all set for the parade. The smallest bear wears a very simple golden wreath—it is just a strip of embossed paper glued to fit around his head with a few gilt sprigs glued to the inside. It took seconds to make—presto, and he's ready to party. The child of nature next to him has a wreath of fresh ivy twisted around a small vine ring, which is whimsically dotted with dried black-eyed Susans. This would be a very sweet wreath for a child to wear on a beautiful day, or if you used fresh flowers, at a wedding. There may be nothing as crazily happy as curling ribbon (a staple of the gift-wrap department), so tie lengths of it to a small wreath form, then pull the edge of your scissor blade from the knot to the end of each one and it will spring into a beautifully silly curl—the more force you use, the tighter the curl will be. The bear on the window ledge wears a wreath made from a paper doily. I simply cut out the center and glued some pictures snipped from magazines to it—you could use stickers as well. (You could use this same idea to make pretty mats for favorite photos.) The little bear on the right is another nature lover. His grapevine wreath sports dried rose leaves and wild rose hips; you could easily get the same effect with artificial trimmings. The birthday bear who is the center of this gathering has transformed a grass wreath into a millinery confection with dried white statice and tiny red roses (I glued these in place, along with the candles.) Please, to avoid tragedy and tears, be very careful with the candles—they're great to light for a quick photo, but then have the guest of honor make a wish and blow them out.

n the springtime the first flowers cause such excitement; they herald the passing of long, cold days with a fresh beauty that I cannot resist. Florists' foam is the least obtrusive of supports and lets me display these freshest of blooms in an almost natural setting. Here I covered a ring of it with fresh eucalyptus berries and variegated ivy. I put a few pink hyacinth blooms into this delicate background and then placed multi-blossomed stems of yellow narcissus and white freesia between them, along with some soft dusty miller leaves. A lavender-and-pink ombré ribbon was woven among the flowers and greens in a rather poetic gesture that seemed appropriate to this admittedly romantic arrangement.

For me, the advent of spring is enough of an occasion to warrant a wreath of this sort, but it would make a lovely centerpiece for Easter, a birthday, or—with seasonal flowers—May Day.

I f you slide a plate beneath a florists' foam ring to catch the water you can make an arrangement upon it that will have the illusion of self-support, almost as if it were growing right out of your table. One Valentine's day I took advantage of this characteristic to make a wreath of fresh roses.

I am partial to the unexpected in wreath making and prefer loose, spontaneous visual surprises and compositional tensions over tightly controlled static designs. I did not want this wreath to be too prim, so first I covered a ring with long sprigs of heather. Their cut ends were inserted into the foam and their tips caught down with brackets of florists' wire; along the circumference they were allowed to spring free in wispy cadence.

I chose an assortment of roses in shades of pink and red, with buds in various states of bloom. As each was placed in the foam at a slightly different angle a pleasing arrangement of colors and textures began to develop. Wanting to add depth to my composition, I filled some of the spaces between the roses with dark purple statice. White baby's breath repeats the delicate theme of the heather and floats in contrast above the deeper colors of the other blooms.

There is a wonderful feeling that comes from working with lavender. I enjoy every moment of contact—growing it, picking it fresh from my summer garden, tying it into small bunches to dry, looking at the color, and breathing the heavenly scent. I often use lavender in my wreath making, especially if I plan to give the wreath away. The fresh scent lingers on my hands and perfumes my workroom while I fashion such a gift; I know and enjoy the extra pleasure a wreath redolent with its beautiful fragrance will bring. I keep a small container of lavender on my worktable, and when the blossoms fall I keep them. Later, I throw some of them into potpourri, but mostly I just enjoy their fragrance while I work. Bunches of lavender are an important part of my design vocabulary, bringing that special muted blue color, which is close to the color of early evening, to any composition. I return often to my own lavender stock until I deplete it, then I go off to the local florist, who always keeps it in the dried-flower section of the shop. As you turn the pages of this book you will find bunches of lavender worked into the design of many wreaths.

To make this little wreath of lavender sprays I first covered a wire ring with Spanish moss. Then I laid the lavender, a few sprigs at a time, counterclockwise against the ring, and wrapped it in place with florists' twine. You'll find as you do this that you must trim the stem ends to follow the curve of the ring as you wrap, otherwise you'll end up with a thick mass of stems that destroys the round shape. To me there is a completeness in the simplicity of this wreath; the variation in the shape and gesture of the lavender sprigs is enough, so I left it unadorned. Perhaps, if it were to be a gift I might add a casual flourish of French ribbon like the one that finishes the heather and rose wreath on page 88, but I think it would be spoiled by anything obviously fancy or ornate.

A lavender wreath makes a lovely topping for a gift box. To avoid crushing the flowers if you use it this way, tie the wreath to the box through the hanging loop. And of course, though really too pretty to hide from view, a lavender wreath will freshen delightfully the inside of a closet or drawer.

When I work with flowers that are very simple and lovely in their own right I often feel that they need very little help from me to be shown to advantage. Here I chose just two pink varieties—dried heather and silica-preserved roses—and arranged them very simply. I think that the trick to this sort of composition is to learn to trust your eye in recognizing when your design has reached the proper proportion—knowing when to stop. I like to use simple designs like this to accent the table when I'm entertaining a few special friends; they also make lovely birthday or "thinking of you" gifts.

The dried heather on this wreath was wrapped onto a wire ring that had been covered with Spanish moss. To begin, I laid a few lengths of heather over the covered ring and wrapped them in place with florists' twine. Working with only a few stems at a time, and placing all the cut ends on the base clockwise, I wrapped on more heather until the ring was covered. I allowed the bloom ends to go their own ways, giving a soft free edge to the wreath while increasing its volume. When the heather was in place I arranged the roses in clusters and attached them with a bit of hot glue.

Once I had placed the wreath in this vignette I added the simple twist of French ribbon because it was so pretty catching the light, but I really feel that the wreath could stand alone in its perfect simplicity. If you were planning to hang a wreath such as this you might want to tie the ribbon in a simple bow as shown on page 131. Whether or not to add a bow is one of those subjective decisions for which there is no right or wrong choice. Sometimes it is important to the occasion or theme of your design to include one—certainly I often do—and sometimes a look at the space where it is to be displayed will make the decision for you.

Whether or not you use a bow, you must never forget to make a loop if you think you might want to hang the wreath. This step should become second nature to you as you gain experience in wreath making, but you may find that for loose, free compositions like this one you may not want to attach the loop—and thus determine the top—until the wreath is completed and you can judge the orientation that is most pleasing.

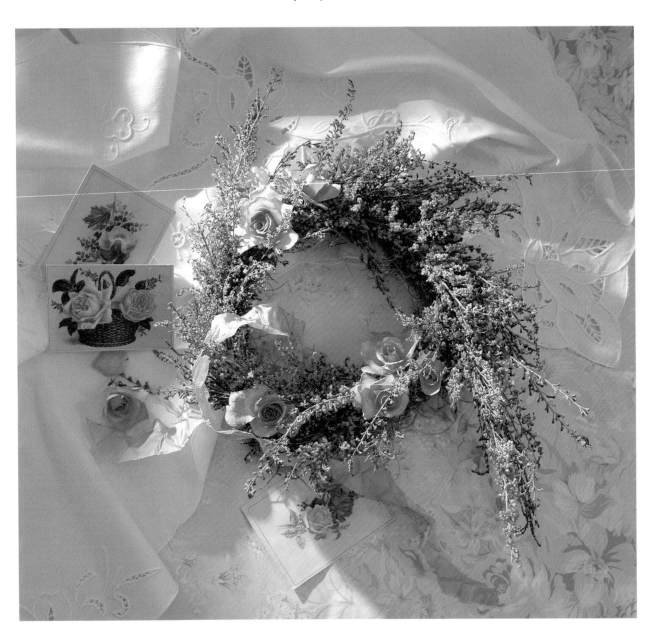

A wreath can be filled with symbolism or any number of abstract meanings. Certain materials evoke specific emotions or memories and carry a direct message to the viewer. Many occasions are associated with colors or flowers that bring forth the feelings or emotions of that moment. Weddings of course are filled with such symbolic associations. Colors, sounds, ceremonies all knit to provide lasting remembrances of one's own wedding or those of friends.

You should never feel restricted when thinking of how a wreath could become part of a special occasion or ceremony, but think creatively and consider using one as a centerpiece, on reception tables or even in smaller proportions as a gift for attendants or guests. This is a wreath that could easily be carried in the wedding party or adapted to hang on the church door to welcome guests.

I began with a simple grapevine base, and wove ivy and dusty miller leaves through it. I put the roses and freesia into water picks and arranged them in a lush crescent, massing some and letting others trail around the circular base, and chose a pearl-edged French ribbon to make the bow. I tucked in a bunch of lavender and some sprays of baby's breath, making the edge light and gracefully loose. (The scent of lavender enhances that of roses; the small bunch used here could be removed and saved as a keepsake.) The combination of fresh ivy, lovely pale roses and freesia, and elegant ribbon is delicate, romantic, and quintessentially bridal.

A small wreath—no more than six or eight inches (15 or 20 cm)—makes a perfect housewarming gift or says a thoughtful thank-you to a hostess. A sample of your creative work is a sincere token but will not overwhelm the recipient. I can't think of a person who would not be happy to find a home for a little wreath of long-lasting dried flowers, such as this one of globe amaranth and roses.

I fashioned this wreath over a straw base and chose to work with blossoms that were all the same color. The globe amaranth were hot-glued in concentric rows that nearly circle the form; to inject a little life into their natural orderliness I left some of the greenery on the stems to peek between the flowers. I wanted to create a focal point at the top of this wreath, so I filled the empty space with dried roses and eucalyptus berries. Then I added some dried rose leaves as a counterpoint to the berries and wispy greens. The French ribbon bow stands in lighthearted authority over the regimented amaranth. Although this wreath has only two colors there are various textures to keep it interesting.

You could make several of these and keep them on hand for those times when a small gift is needed. Globe amaranth is a very sturdy flower, so they will store well if wrapped in tissue and boxed so as not to jostle the roses.

CHAPTER

3

NEW IDEAS
AND MATERIALS

I t is not always necessary to have a vision of the wreath you want to create before you choose your materials. Sometimes, the materials will suggest the design, but slowly, one element at a time. It can be interesting to choose a few diverse pieces, then experiment until they come together into a coherent design.

With this wreath, for instance, I started by selecting an odd assortment of ingredients with no clear idea of how they would fit together: silk leaves, artificial berries, wire, acrylic and metallic paints, and Dutch Metal (a synthetic metal leaf). I started by shaping the wire into several rings, which I covered with florists' tape. Then, one at a time, I put the wreaths together; using very fine florists' wire, I wrapped each leaf stem onto the ring and then covered the wire wrap with florists' tape. Continuing to work in this manner, I added successive leaves and berries until the pattern was complete. I decided that each of the variations should have a different surface treatment, so I began to color the leaves and berries. The simple leaves gave the wreaths a feeling of classical antiquity and I emphasized this by giving each group a metallic patina with the Dutch Metal and the paints. I always enjoy experimenting with paint; each experiment produces another result, and I am always questing for ways to imitate the patina of aged and weathered metals. One word of caution, though: when painting fabric leaves you must be careful not to saturate them or the glue that holds them to their wire stems will dissolve and all your work will be for naught.

Very often the most successful design is the most spontaneous, the one that just happens because the creator is having fun, relaxing, and immersing himself in the experience.

This free-spirited wreath was made in just such a lighthearted mood. There is really nothing to it, but it has a wonderful, easy energy and, with the gold surface, is at the same time elegant and rather amusing. All I did here was wire a loose composition of leaves, pinecones, acorns, and artificial berries to a wire ring that I had wrapped with florists' tape. When each element was in place I stood back, took a look, moved a few pieces, looked again to be sure the balance of elements seemed right and the overall rhythm interesting, and then wrapped ev-

erything securely in place with florists' tape. Then I gave the entire wreath a coating of gold spray paint. That's all, except that I poked in a few colorful insects—those wonderful metal pins you can buy in novelty shops—that are both beautiful and funny in the golden wilderness.

Any time you make a design in this sort of mood you should feel free to let it lead you wherever it will. You could go on from this point and add another metallic spray to highlight some part of the arrangement or you could use nonmetallic paint instead of the gold. If you were in a whimsical mood you might want to include small objects other than berries and pinecones—or metal bugs—with a meaning sentimental to you. Use your imagination and trust your instincts.

ince I've said so often that you should look around your environment to see what sort of materials are available, it should come as no surprise that I used this bit of old rusted fencing to make a wreath. It made me think of wagon trains and Old West trails. I carefully rolled it into this open wreath and tied a few scraps of old fabric onto the coils.

Displayed outdoors like this, the wreath is a bit of environmental sculpture. I could see it working as well in the right sort of house, one that is either very rustic or very modern and open, where the stark wire form would stand out against the walls. In a sophisticated environment the wreath might be transformed from a lonely cowpoke artifact to a modern-age montage; this idea could be emphasized by the addition of other abstract metal and wire shapes. If you are more interested in the narrative attributes that first attracted me to the fence, you could include a horseshoe or some cut tin elements that would reiterate the history and, aesthetically, the *metalness* of the wreath. If you wanted to display this at Christmastime you could include some Mexican tin ornaments, perhaps aging them first with paint as I did on page 62.

While not everyone has access to an abandoned and beautifully rusted wire fence, there are other ways in which this concept could be executed. Over time, new, non-galvanized metal will corrode and rust if it's left unprotected outdoors. There are also products that you can purchase at craft supply stores that will give metal an antique patina.

R ecently I have spent some time drawing the architectural embellishments I see on old buildings. What makes them appealing to me is the complex and imaginative use of ornament by the designers and craftsmen who built them. The juxtaposition of imagery and the varying scale of the ornament add drama and mystery to the scrolls and swags that connect and define windows, grace cornices, or make up great corbels. As I worked on the drawings I started to play around with the idea of making a very sculptural, high-relief wreath with a design built from disparate three-dimensional objects and unified by a surface coating—so it would appear to be carved in stone. There is a wonderful spray-on medium called Stone Fleck that gives exactly that effect; it is available in several stonelike colors at crafts supply stores and is extremely easy to use.

In composing this wreath I was most interested in the sculptural qualities and relative scale of my materials; their natural color and texture would be obscured by the coating medium, and I chose to ignore any narrative relationship they might or might not have. So I looked for objects that were very dimensional with interesting shapes, or that had deeply scored surfaces. Seashells naturally fall into this category, as do fruits, so I pulled things from my shell and sand dollar collection and my boxes of artificial fruits and berries, and added a few dried pomegranates and blown goose eggs to them. I glued all of these onto a foam base, piling them up on one another in a pattern of subtle twists and turns, and using the flat but incised sand dollars and scallop shells to add balance to the roundness of the eggs and fruit. When I felt that the arrangement had the complexity I had seen in the architectural carvings, I sprayed it with the Stone Fleck, which erased the individuality of the component parts. By using a darker tone of Stone Fleck at the circumference and a lighter one toward the center, I intensified the shadows and heightened the effect of sculptural relief.

These sunflowers were created for me by the talented hands of Fred Sutton, whose wonderful silk flowers are not mere replicas but new expressions of understood forms. In making this spectacular wreath I simply recreated one I often make when I finish the day's sunflower harvest, but these flowers will happily keep their magnificent petals and rich color for an indefinite time. Adding one flower at a time, I just twisted the ample wire stems together to form a vinelike structure that supported the lovely heads. When the circle was complete I reinforced the shape with tape-covered florists' wire, making the hanging loop at the same time.

When you make a wreath by twisting the stems of artificial flowers into a ring you usually want the stems to be as long as possible so that the shape is sturdy, so don't trim any excess until you are pleased with your composition. (When you are ready to trim, use strong wire cutters, not pruners.) If the stems are too short to work with in this manner, you can lengthen them by overlapping some heavy florists' wire on them and covering it with florists' tape. If on the other hand you want to make a wreath of fresh sunflowers you will need to use a base of some sort, as the natural stems are neither strong nor flexible enough to twist together. I often take a length of freshly cut vine and twist it into a loose, open wreath, and then secure the heavy blooms to it with wire ties. Bear in mind that while fresh sunflowers are spectacularly beautiful, they fade quickly when cut; hang them inside until they fade, then put them outside for the birds to enjoy.

Silk flowers have a great appeal to many people; they are long lasting, easy to work with, and readily available. If skillfully arranged, they can be as beautiful as their fresh counterparts. I thought it would be interesting to develop a wreath from them that was a reflection of Flemish still-life painting—where artists composed marvelous, sensuous arrangements of diverse flowers—and I asked Fred Sutton, a floral designer whose skilled fingers work bits of fabric and wire into the most poetic creations, to make an overblown bouquet with which I could re-create that sort of luxurious canvas.

My feeling when I saw Fred's flowers was that he had captured beautifully the loose, organic qualities of the originals. This was perfect for the seventeenth-century-inspired still-life I wanted to compose, where every element should be as free and natural as possible. I decided to begin with an equally organic grapevine base, and wove ivy and other foliage through it. I arranged the various flowers into a lush crescent, massing some and letting others trail around the circular base, making

the edge light and gracefully loose. By constantly juxtaposing bright or light colors against darker ones, the wreath became a tapestry with a depth and energy that echoed the luxurious sensuality of my historical inspiration.

Design inspiration can be found nearly anywhere. My creative thoughts are always sent into a whirl when I look at the work of designers and artists of the past who have left so many rich interpretations of the world they saw. I think of the mood and message that I find in each artist's work and try to understand what it is about it that evokes the response that I feel, and then wonder how my work can be shaped to evoke similar feelings. When you choose the work of a specific period or artist as your inspiration, and develop a piece in compliment to it, you truly begin to understand the original. Whether you mimic or interpret, you must work through the elements that make up the composition, a challenge that is not only useful in a very instructional way, it is fascinating—and so important in helping you to find your own style.

ot all wreaths need to be serious intellectual endeavors. Some should be made in a spirit of fun, just to capture a bit of fresh air or lightheartedness. While the amount of time necessary to see such an idea through is always unpredictable, sometimes inspiration hits you and everything falls right into place, which was the case with this whimsical construction. One thing important to remember in wreath making—as in so many activities—is to allow yourself to follow your creative impulses and have fun.

Two feathered birds sit upon the exposed vine of this amusing wreath; they gaze into a pint box filled with strawberries. A few small clumps of lichen help anchor the artificial ivy to the wreath and support the eucalyptus berries and tiny clusters of tansy. A fresh green French ribbon brightens up the muted colors and guides the eye from bird to bird. The few elements used on this wreath were assembled with hot glue; the composition went together effortlessly—with immediate satisfaction.

rench ribbon is one of the loveliest and most versatile of materials. I work with it often—turn the pages of this book and you see it in diverse situations. It comes in the most wonderful subtle and saturated colors, it is made of crisp, reflective tafetta, and it has wired edges that allow it to hold any shape; it really has all the picture-perfect qualities you dream of ribbons having and is simply a joy to use.

In making this wreath I wanted to exploit all those wonderful characteristics in a design that was lush, rich, sensual—and frivolous. I began by wrapping an oval form with wide magenta ribbon, securing the tails on the back with pins. Then I tied bows of several related colors and different widths, which I arranged exuberantly on the form, pinning or gluing them in place. I twisted, scrunched, and trailed the wired ribbon so that it bounces light and catches the eye in a most engaging manner.

There are as many ways to use this technique as there are colors and widths of ribbon. It would be lovely in seasonal colors, or elegant in contrasting ones. You could create a rainbow effect or simply complement the palette of your setting. However you might choose to interpret the concept, the ribbon will lead your eye through a dance of color, light, and shadow.

here are no rules saying that wreaths should be made only from specific materials. As a designer, you can choose to work with any material that appeals to you; you will simply adjust your eye and perhaps your technique to accommodate variations in scale or permanence. So keep your eyes open and recognize the potential in nontraditional materials.

A birch tree had fallen on my property and I was cutting it up to fashion into some odd little tables for my porch when it occurred to me to arrange some of the logs into a rustic wreath. I studied them to discover the natural bends and arches that could be reconfigured into a ring. Taking advantage of these, I laid out the logs, letting them overlap and extend as necessary to make a circle whose propor-

tion was pleasing. After doing some jockeying and shifting to get the shape as I wished, I trimmed any excess that seemed out of balance. Then I pre-drilled holes where the logs overlapped and screwed them together. You could also nail this construction together, but whichever method you choose, be sure to make the joints sturdy, as they are all that holds the logs in the shape you have created. (I have used this same procedure to construct twig wreaths, allowing the natural curves of the twigs to dictate the flow and gesture of the shape, which tends to be more aggressive since the twigs are more complex.)

When you hang a log wreath you will want to consider the relationship of its visual weight to the display space. Of course, you don't need to have a gazebo—try a garden fence, the eaves of a rustic shed, or a porch column. If you have the right sort of home, you might even want to hang it indoors.

lthough the design of a wreath should always complement the physical qualities of its surface, there is nothing to say that you cannot create that surface. I often cover a foam shape with a material such as moss that softens and disguises in a rather unobtrusive way, or build up a whole new surface with individual dimensional elements such as pinecones or dried flowers. Here I wanted to create a very quick, loose covering that belied the solidity of its support and then, by embellishing it with dimensional but related materials, give it a cohesive substance. My concept was to wrap a base with fabric, which can create movement as it folds and drapes, and then to trim it with a like but not identical material. In this instance I chose to work with raffia cloth and raffia-covered fruit shapes, but there are infinite ways in which this fabric-wrapping concept could be used; whatever fabric you might choose will completely change the design. The important things to understand when approaching something like this are just how varied the possibilities are and that your own expression of them will bring you the most rewarding satisfaction.

Raffia is the dominant material in this autumn wreath. It provides the overall color and primary texture. I cut a length of raffia cloth and wrapped it loosely around the base, tying it with strands of raffia in four places. The sectional ties stand out from the surface, amplifying the twisted motion of the wrapped form. I purchased the large raffia-wrapped apples in a craft supply store thinking they would be at home in this nearly monochrome design. (They would be easy to construct from scratch if you had sufficient Styrofoam to carve the shapes from and enough raffia to wrap them with.) I placed them at the bottom of the wreath and built a nest for them by tucking bleached yucca pods, some warmer-colored coxcomb, and black beard wheat into the folds of the fabric. I added some sprays of little wild rose hips to break up the beige and superimpose some sprightliness on the heavier apple forms. They seem to dance among the elements, carrying the eye from shape to shape.

his playful wreath is wonderful to have for a children's party. The kids can make the flowers and help develop the theme of the remaining decorations; perhaps bright straw hats, a piñata, and votive candles for the table. Making the flowers is a perfect afternoon's project; they are very easy and almost nothing could be faster (one person can make enough for a wreath like this in about two hours). All you need are a few colors of crepe paper (start with packs of folded sheets rather than rolls), a few lengths of florists' wire, some three-inch (7.5-cm) florists' picks, and a straw wreath base. If you like, you can add a few half-yard lengths of brightly colored double-faced satin ribbon; they make a fun finishing touch and add to the carnival mood.

Take the crepe paper out of its wrapper but leave it folded. For the central "petals", cut a three-inch (7.5-cm) wide strip across the end of one color paper, unfold it, and cut off a six-inch (15cm) length. For the outer petals of the flower, cut a three-inch (7.5-cm) wide strip from contrasting paper. To begin, gather up one edge of the central-petal paper, holding it in one hand and feeding it between the thumb and first finger of your other hand. (I hold the paper in my left hand and feed it into my right.) Once the crepe paper is gathered in your hand, secure it with a length of florists' wire. Unfold the outer-petal strip of paper and gather it up around the first, turning the whole unit in your hand as you gather and wrap. It is not important to do this with symmetrical care or great precision, as the flower should have an erratic, cheerful spirit. When all the paper is gathered up, secure it around the center with another piece of florists' wire. Then wire it onto the florists' pick and set aside. If you do not wish to have a contrasting color center, omit the first part of the process. Make as many flowers as you wish, in as many colors as you please.

Before poking the flowers into place, I covered this wreath form with a single color of crepe paper, wrapping it around the ring. This ensured that it would look finished from any angle; it is not an essential step. I also made a few smaller flowers to mix with the larger ones. They add interest and rhythm to the arrangement of similarly sized forms. Once the flowers were on the base, I added the ribbons, wired onto florists' picks.

When you have weekend guests, make them feel at home with a selection of toiletries. While it is easy enough to put these in a basket on the guest bath vanity, it is more personal—and more fun—to tie them onto a wreath. I usually buy an assortment of travel-size products from one company so that the packaging makes a coordinated array, and then just tie them onto a straw or vine wreath with pretty curling ribbon. If I want my guest to keep the wreath as a memento of the visit, I'll add some clusters of lavender or dried flowers tied with raffia or ribbon, or perhaps cover the base with moss and tiny blossoms, so that the wreath will be pretty once the toiletries have been removed. Sometimes I'll make up one of the small wreaths seen in this book and use it to ring the soaps and shampoos, or tie it to a basket that holds them.

If you are a collector of hotel soaps, matchbooks, or even decorative sugar packets, you might like to use this idea to make a sentimental or whimsical wreath to perch where it will catch your eye from time to time. Or give it to a child or friend to whom you have promised a souvenir from your vacation. This is a simple idea with many possible variations, any one would make a thoughtful gesture.

Winter is a perfectly wonderful time to make a bird-feeding wreath. Filled with purchased seed bells or homemade shapes cut from rendered suet, sunflowers saved from the garden, and fruits and wild berries, such a wreath attracts feathered friends while delighting human observers with its simple aesthetics. I find that once the birds grow accustomed to a wreath near my home, those who are naturally bold will also come to my hand for feeding; I simply place a few seeds in my palm and stand as still as a garden ornament, within a few minutes they light on my fingers and dine. Children and city guests are thrilled with this pastime.

A small feeding wreath would be a terrific gift for a child (or a large one for a classroom), allowing small fry to watch the activities of nature at close range and giving them a sense of importance as they keep replenishing the disappearing food.

Each winter I make my neighborhood birds a wreath of evergreens wired onto a loose grapevine base and fill it with eatables that I know they particularly enjoy. Every autumn I set aside a few sunflower heads for just this purpose. From my local nursery I purchase seed bells and small bags of select seeds such as corn, thistle, or millet. I purchase suet from the local supermarket, which I slice, cut into heart or star shapes with a cookie cutter, and press into a mixture of seeds. Some shapes I cover with just one specific seed; with their individual colors and textures these look very nice clustered against the fresh mixed greens, and each attracts a particular kind of bird. In addition to the suet and seeds, I hang slices of citrus and clusters of grapes, rose hips, and any other wild berries I can

find on the wreath. If I have a string of cranberries on my Christmas tree I will save it and intertwine it with the boughs.

When finished I hang the wreath where I have a good view of it; it is surprising how close I can place it to my house. Then it is terrific to sit by a window and observe the mix of birds that comes to feed upon the various treats. This is such a simple and inexpensive wreath to make, yet it brings an enormous amount of pleasure to so many creatures.

CHAPTER

4

TECHNIQUES AND WORKING HABITS

GATHERING NATURAL MATERIALS

Throughout this book I speak of materials gathered from the woods around my home. I am lucky to live deep in the countryside, but not everyone shares this privilege. Most of the materials I use in wreath making can be purchased from a good florist or craft supply shop. If you don't know the name of something, perhaps your florist will recognize it if shown a photo.

If you do go foraging, be respectful of the environment. Some plants are considered endangered in certain areas, so check with your county agricultural extension service or local DEC office to see if there is anything that should not be harvested. And be aware that the birds really do like to eat bittersweet, juniper, and other berries—these may actually be depleted or less than picture-perfect when you go to cut them. And of course, do everything possible to avoid trespassing, and watch for poison ivy. Otherwise, enjoy your time in the outdoors and always be open to nature's inspiration.

SETTING UP A WORK SPACE

Wreath making is most pleasurably done with the proper tools in adequate space. This is not to say that you cannot make the most spectacular arrangements in conditions that are less than perfect, but the better your work area, the more smoothly your efforts will proceed. Of course, the sophistication of your work area will depend on the space and perhaps funds available to you, and it is possible to work successfully on the kitchen table.

The most essential thing is that you have a clear space with as few interruptive obstacles as possible. Basically, you need two surfaces to work on—one vertical, one horizontal. I prefer a wall when making most of my designs, but some can only be developed on a tabletop. In my studio, I have a nail firmly embedded in a wall that is perpendicular to my table. I can pivot directly from one surface to the other. I have sufficient room to step back and see how a wreath is developing on the wall, and yet I am close enough to my worktable to have all the necessary tools and supplies at hand. I also have a large metal shelf unit at the far end of my worktable that holds boxes of supplies and dried materials. Another wall is covered with pegboard, which is great not only for storing tools but handy for hanging wreaths in various stages of completion.

Your work area should be well lighted by both nature and electricity, and ideally the light sources should be such that there are no shadows falling on your work. I use inexpensive clip-on lights as they are easy to move around, allowing me to adjust the light so it is always even. It is also very important to have electrical outlets nearby, as you will no doubt often use a hot-glue gun and perhaps other light tools, and it is frustrating and dangerous to maneuver around long extension cords.

If you are able to set up a permanent work area, try to make your table a comfortable height—at the hip bone is ideal; this will save your back and shoulders from strain. My table is simply a piece of plywood on two sawhorses, so it is easy to break down or even move outdoors.

No work area ever has enough storage space, but try to arrange as much as you can. Wire or metal industrial shelving is functional, fairly inexpensive, and easy to assemble or adjust. I gather and save all sorts of boxes that I fill, label clearly, and stack on the shelves. If you can afford it, consider ordering uniform storage boxes from an office supplier, they are most efficient. Plastic storage boxes are important for holding dried materials.

TOOLS AND SUPPLIES

For gathering materials in the wild, I always carry a good pair of garden *pruners* and a sharp *pocketknife*, both of which can be slipped into my pocket. I often carry a small *saw* as well; I have one that fits into a sheath I strap onto my belt. I also have a light bow saw with a blade protector. *Scissors* or floral *shears* can be handy to have along as well.

In my work room I have *wire cutters, scissors* for fabric and ribbon, and second pairs of *pruners* and floral *shears*. I have a couple of *hot-glue guns*; my favorite is the kind with a trigger to regulate the flow, which gives me better control and more freedom of movement.

Craft or florists' wire is used to attach various materials to one another and to make new stems for dried flowers, if necessary. It also makes the hanging loop for each wreath. It is a good idea to stock several weights of wire.

Florists' picks are small wood sticks with a thin wire at one end. They come in either natural or green in a variety of lengths. You can wrap the wire around one of your decorative elements and then stick the other end of the pick right into a foam or straw wreath base. *Water picks* are tubes that hold fresh flowers or greens; they are easiest to use with vine wreaths. Picks let you design quickly and flexibly in many situations. I keep a large supply on hand at all times.

I also keep a supply of *florists' tape* in green and brown, colors that blend with most of my materials. The tape can be wrapped over wire stems, strengthening and disguising them.

In addition to these, all of which are available at a good craft or florists' supply shop, I have quite an assortment of *glues* and *paints*. Quick-drying white glue is the most important adhesive after the pellets for the glue gun; there are others you will no doubt acquire as you work. I use acrylic and metallic paints from time to time, so I also have assorted *paint brushes*; sometimes I even use *dye* to color dried cones or vines. Another thing that is very handy to have is *twine* or *string*; I keep garden, kitchen, and waxed types around.

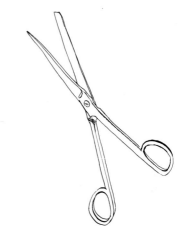

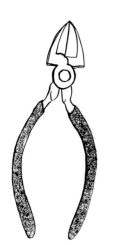

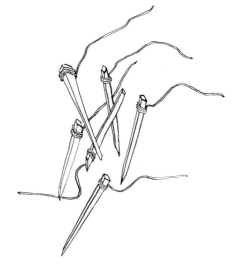

Illustrations by: Madeline Sorel

WREATH BASES YOU CAN PURCHASE

Most of the wreaths I make begin on a form of one sort or another. Sometimes I weave or twist vines into a ring, but very often I use a purchased base.

Vine wreaths are widely available in a broad range of sizes. They are usually made of grapevine, but sometimes you find them made of honeysuckle or other materials, sometimes even paper rope. They come in natural and many other colors and in a variety of densities. You can also find them in heart shapes in many sizes. When I work with a vine wreath it is almost always one of my design elements; I intend for it to be seen and work with its character rather than completely covering it with other elements.

Straw wreath bases also come in many sizes and several shapes. These are made of dense straw wrapped with nylon filament over a wire ring; they are tight and full. You can use them as you find them or cover the surface with moss, and you can poke things into them or glue directly onto the straw. Very small wreaths of this type are sometimes made of grass.

Foam wreath bases are similar to straw ones; they are easy to work on, but you will most likely want to completely obscure their surface when you use them. They can be made of cut or extruded foam; the former have flat surfaces, the latter have rounded edges and are usually reinforced with wire and will hold heavier embellishments. You can also buy bases of Oasis™, a florists' foam that is sponge-like and will hold water; it is ideal for making fresh flower wreaths.

Wire bases can be made of one or several rings or heart shapes and also come in many sizes. They are very good for making wreaths of fresh flowers or greens as it is easy to twine things through them, it is also easy to attach things to them with wire, though not with glue. You have to be careful with wire rings to make a composition that is full enough to obscure the understructure.

SOME BASIC STEPS

When you begin to work on a design, it is a good idea to gather the materials you plan to use and make a rough arrangement just to see if you have everything you need and get a good idea of the techniques you will be using. If you realize that something is missing, try to find it before you become immersed in the creative work so you will not be interrupted later.

The first step in making almost any wreath is to attach a *wire hanging loop* to the base. Take a length of florists' wire, pass it through the center of the wreath and bring the ends together at the perimeter. Twist them together and circle them back on themselves, twisting again to form a sturdy loop. This establishes the top of your design and lets you hang the wreath while you are working on it. It can be quite difficult to try to sneak a loop through the embellishments once the design is finished; I do this only in rare cases where for some aesthetic reason I cannot choose the top until the arrangement is complete.

There are two ways to *cover a wreath base* with a background material such as moss. If you are working on a straw or foam base, you can simply glue the moss in place with hot glue or quick-drying craft glue *(A).* Don't try to cover the entire base at once;

A.

B.

work with one conveniently sized piece of covering at a time, applying glue to the wrong side and pressing it onto the base.

If you are working with a wire base or a covering that would be awkward to glue (or don't want the covering to be permanent), you can wrap the covering on a spool of twine *(B)*. Pass one end of the twine through the center of the wreath and tie it securely to itself around the base, placing the knot on the back of the base. Lay a piece of the covering over the base and wrap the twine through the center and over the base to secure it; place the wraps of twine only as close together as necessary to hold the material in place. Continue in this manner until you have covered the base, then tie the twine to itself on the back. When you place decorative elements on a background that has been wrapped to the base, be sure to arrange them so that the twine is covered.

To *mask florists' wire* so that it looks natural and stemlike, cover it with florists' tape *(C)*. Hold the tape in your left hand and with your right hand place the wire at an angle against it. With your right thumb and forefinger, twist the tape over the wire, then spin the wire against the tape, winding the tape over it until it is covered. With a little practice this motion will become second nature. If you insert one end of the wire into a short flower stem (or hold it next to it if it won't slide inside) before

C.

D.

E.

you wrap the wire you can attach them together in one motion—just be sure to begin wrapping at the flower—thus *giving a flower a new stem.*

You can use a spool of twine to *wrap decorative materials onto a base (D)* in much the same manner that you wrap on a background covering, wrapping the twine several times over each element so that it is very secure. All of your materials should have stems long enough to lie flat against the base and be held by the twine. Small elements can be wired together into bunches; those that are large or full can be applied singly—large bunches are awkward to work with and will not give graceful results. When wrapping materials onto a wreath, it is very important to have a plan in mind since, once you start wrapping, it is almost impossible to go back and add another element. As you arrange your materials all of the stems must face in roughly the same direction—either clockwise or counterclockwise; you can adjust the angle at which you place them to slant toward the center or perimeter of the wreath and thus create a full surface. You needn't worry about using too many flowers or greens; a full wreath is always lovely and you don't want to risk leaving the mechanics exposed.

Begin by passing one end of the twine through the center of the wreath and tying it securely to itself around the base, placing the knot on the back. Place your first embellishment on the base and wrap the twine through the center and over the base several times to secure it, then add another embellishment. Continue in this manner around the wreath; when you approach the beginning, carefully slide the stems of the last embellishments under the first and wrap very gently. When you are finished, tie off the twine on the back of the wreath. Occasionally I find that in spite of my cares to plan ahead, there is a hole somewhere in the design; when this happens I wire another bit of embellishment onto a pick and insert it into the wreath.

Use florists' picks to *insert materials into a wreath base (E)*. Wrap the wire on the pick around the material until it is secure, then poke the other end of the pick into the base. You can attach just one element to a pick, or cluster several together as you wish. You can twine the wire through the scales of a pinecone or the knot of a bow, or simply poke the end of the pick into a piece of fruit or a foam object. Sometimes you may find it necessary to use glue to attach a pick to either an embellishment or a wreath base.

Use water picks when you want to have *an accent of fresh flowers in a wreath.* These are small, pointed glass or plastic tubes that have a rubber cap with a small hole over the open end. You fill them with water, cap them, and insert the flower stem, then tuck them into your wreath. If you replenish the water the flowers should last for several days.

HOW TO MAKE A VINE WREATH

Making a vine wreath is really very simple. Hold one end of a length of vine in your left hand, and with your right hand bend the vine into a circle the diameter of the wreath you wish to make; with your left hand, clasp the vine where it overlaps. With your right hand, wrap the free end of the vine in and out through the circle, and secure the end by tucking it into the interstices. Add a second length of vine, tucking it into the first and wrapping it in and out of the circle as before. As you continue to add vines the wreath will grow in thickness and become increasingly dense and sturdy. When the wreath is the size you desire, you can tuck in any stray ends if you wish; sometimes I like to leave the

bits that trail and spring free around the surface.

You can also make a wreath working with three lengths of vine at once. Hold them together and twist them into a single rope, then work with them in the manner described above.

Although wrapping a vine wreath is fairly easy, it is important to pay attention to how tight your work is. The degree of firmness or looseness will help to determine the look of your ultimate design. I almost always make my wreaths very full, and prefer them to be somewhat irregular rather than perfectly even. This provides me with more unexpected surfaces to embellish and allows me to discover that element of surprise I mention so often.

HOW TO DRY FLOWERS AND GREENS

Most flowers can be dried by one or both of two simple methods—air-drying or silica preserving. The results will vary with the flower type and humidity; drying time and color retention may be different for the same flower with the different methods. While it is impossible to give precise instructions for either method, both are worth experimenting with—particularly if you garden.

Air-drying is a simple way to preserve fresh flowers. Pick them after any dew has evaporated, when the sun has begun to warm the earth. Strip their leaves and tie them into bunches of three to five stems. Hang the bunches upside down in a dry, dust-free, dimly lit place such as an attic or closet. Alternatively, you can hang each bunch inside a paper bag. You can also spread flowers or greens on a screen to dry in your attic; just be sure that air can circulate all around it.

Check the flowers after a couple of days. The precise drying time will depend upon the type of flower and the temperature and humidity. When the petals feel like paper and are no longer soft and pliable, they should be transferred to airtight storage containers, such as plastic sweater boxes. To assure that they will be good looking when you are ready to use them, keep them away from moisture and direct sunlight.

Silica gel is a desiccating powder that will remove the moisture from fresh flowers; it is sand-like in texture and can be purchased at most craft supply stores. To dry flowers in it you need an airtight plastic container (a sweater box is ideal), a small bowl or measuring cup to hold the gel while you work with it, and a slotted spoon. For best results, the stems on the flowers should be cut to no more than 1 inch (2.5cm).

The gel is very dusty, so pour it slowly. Fill the container about two-thirds full with the silica gel. Lay each blossom in the gel, face up. Gently sprinkle additional gel around and over the blossoms, filling in between all the petals. Cover the flowers completely. Put the cover on the box and set it aside. Check the flowers after three days; three or four days is enough to dry most flowers but those with heavy stems or thick petals may take longer.

When the flowers are dry, they tend to be fragile and sometimes break apart when they are handled, so be very careful removing them from the gel. The best way to do this is to brush some gel away from a blossom, slide a slotted spoon under it, and remove it gently; don't try to remove more than one blossom at a time. Store them in another plastic box, placing a thin layer of gel in the bottom.

When you are ready to work with them, you can wire new stems onto the blossoms with florists' tape. Should any petals fall off through handling, use white glue applied with a small paint brush to put them back in place.

HOW TO WORK WITH FLORISTS' FOAM

Florists' foam is a hard, dense, sponge-like material that, when wetted, retains moisture for a substantial period of time. When you insert the stems of fresh flowers or greens into moist florists' foam, they drink the water and remain as fresh as they would in a vase; it's a wonderful material to use for center-pieces or other arrangements where you might find that a vase is too high or just not the right propor-tion for the effect you have in mind. To protect the surface on which it will sit, place the florists' foam on or in a waterproof container; if this is not a concern—for instance, you want to arrange flowers in a hanging basket outdoors—it will hold moisture for some time without obviously dripping. Check your arrangement for moistness every few days and replenish the water if necessary.

If you have never tried to work with florists' foam you will find it gives you all sorts of freedom. It comes in bricks that you can cut or wire together to make any shape or size you desire. For wreath making it also comes in rings of various sizes. Because florists' foam is so firm, it acts like a florists' frog and gives you complete control over the shape of an arrangement. It is ideal to use when working with flowers that have very short stems, like wild roses, difficult to arrange in vases. Dampen the florists' foam and then simply insert the stems of your flowers and greens directly in it *(A and B)*.

A.

B.

TRIMMING WITH BOWS

Tying a bow on a wreath can be as simple as tying your shoe *(A, B, and C)*. Some ribbons will hold a shape better than others. French ribbon, which has wired edges, is the easiest to control, but there are many other types, each of which has its uses.

Sometimes it is easier to control the shape of a bow if you "tie" it before you put it on the wreath. Often bows are contrived from several shorter lengths of ribbon that are folded and twisted into shapes secured with wire; the ends of the wire are then used to attach the bow to the wreath *(D, E, and F)*.

To make it appear that a wreath is hanging from a bow, tie a loop of ribbon over the wire hanging loop, then pin a pretied ribbon bow onto the top of it (twist the wire loop to poke out behind the ribbon one) *(G and H)*.

A.

B.

C.

F.

D.

G.

E.

H.

SURFACE TREATMENTS

Some designers spray their dried floral wreaths with a *clear sealer* that coats the surface of all the blooms. They do this to preserve the arrangement and make dusting easier. I prefer to keep my work natural and refrain from using clear lacquers or sprays. I would rather enjoy a flower for a shorter time than stiffen it with a glaze. To store a wreath between seasons, gently wrap it in tissue paper, put it in a box, and place it where it won't get bumped until you are ready to use it again.

Leaves, pinecones, and similar materials, on the other hand, can be fun to transform with *paint* or even *gloss medium*. You can totally cover their surface with color, which gives them a completely new look, or just touch the edges or spines to emphasize a natural detail. You can also buy leaves that have been *preserved* (usually in glycerin), and these have a glossy look that is appealing in certain designs.

Dutch Metal—thin squares of imitation silver or gold leaf—is available at art or craft supply stores. It gives a richer luminosity to a surface than paint, which tends to be flat and opaque, it is also easier to control than spray paint would be. All you have to do to use it is to prepare the surface of whatever you wish to leaf with some sort of adhesive (white glue works well), then gently press sheets of the metallic leaf onto the glue with a brush or your fingers and, once the glue has set, brush off the excess leaf *(A and B).* You can get interesting effects if you combine the silver and gold or if you apply them to selective areas of the object you are working with. There is something wonderfully Old World about metallic leaf; it adds a festive sparkle to even the most ordinary objects.

A.

B.

HOW TO SUGAR FRUIT

The materials you will need are few: two lightly beaten egg whites in a medium-size bowl; a pastry or paintbrush; another medium-size bowl with a cup of granulated sugar; a wire rack; some paper towels, and a moist sponge.

Cover your work surface with paper towels. Select a piece of fruit and hold it as delicately as possible in the fingers of one hand. Using the brush, coat it lightly with egg white. (Sugared fruit dries with a hard coat; if necessary you can touch up any missed areas or finger prints once your fruit is arranged.) With your fingers, sprinkle sugar over the coated fruit. If you feel that the sugarcoating is too thick, wipe it off with the damp sponge and try again. Set the fruit on the wire rack to dry, about thirty to sixty minutes, depending on the humidity. Repeat until you have sugared as many pieces of fruit as desired.

I have made sugared fruit using white glue instead of egg white as the adhesive. It works just as well but is not quite as translucent. Sometimes I add a bit of fine glitter to the sugar; it picks up light and gives an extra sparkle to the fruit. There is no reason why you couldn't skip the sugar altogether and just cover the fruit with a light dusting of glitter. I think however that the effect of the sugar on the fruit is somehow more magical; the subtle coloration of each piece blushes through the crystals in a truly festive transformation of the ordinary.

Sources

Most of the materials used to make the wreaths in this book are readily available at retail stores. Contact the following suppliers for assistance with a local source if there is something that you cannot locate easily.

ARROW FASTENER CO., INC.
271 Mayhill Street
Saddlebrook, NJ 07662
201/843-6900
hot glue gun

ARTIS, INC.
PO Box 407
Solvang, CA 93463
800/688-7339
800/457-0523
craft glues

BOB'S CANDY, INC.
PO Box 3170
Albany, GA 31708
912/435-2121
Christmas candies

BRIMAR, INC.
1706 Marcee Lang
PO Box 2621
Northbrook, IL 60065-9585
708/272-9585
metallic cording and trims

FRED SUTTON
229 West 4th Street
New York, NY 10014
212/627-7641
silk flowers

HALLMARK CARDS
2501 McGee
Box 419580
Kansas City, MO 64141-6580
816/274-8272
candles and party goods

JUST ACCENTS
225 Fifth Avenue
Suite 1121
New York, NY 10010
212/889-3088
ribbon

KISS MY FACE SOAPS
PO Box 224
Gardiner, NY 12525
914/255-0884
toiletries

KNUD NIELSEN
PO Box 746
Evergreen, AL 36401
800/633-1682
dried materials and accessories

MPR ASSOCIATES
PO Box 7343
High Point, NC 27264
800/334-1047
Creative Twist paper ribbon

OFFRAY RIBBONS
Route 24
Chester, NJ 07930-0601
201/879-4700
ribbon

PANGAEA
5 Pine Hill Avenue
Norwalk, CT 06855
203/855-1295
Mexican tin ornaments

R. ROSS & SONS NURSERY
Box 125A
Kingston, NY 12401
914/338-8023

SEAGROATT FLORAL
107 Champlain Street
Albany, NY 12204
800/888-3597
fresh and dried roses

STONE FLECK
410 North Michigan Avenue
Suite 1080
Chicago, IL 60611
312/670-0470
stonelike spray-on finish

THUMBPRINT ANTIQUES
Old Tongore Road
Stone Ridge, NY 10142
914/687-9318
antiques

VABAN RIBBONS
INTERNATIONAL
225 Fifth Avenue
Suite 1121
New York, NY 10010
212/889-3088
ribbon

Index